Great Chefs Draw Inspiration from the Dutch Masters

The Rijksmuseum Cookbook

Great Chefs Draw Inspiration from the Dutch Masters

The Rijksmuseum Cookbook

Bert Natter

Translated from the Dutch by

Sam Garrett and Dagmar Speer

Thomas Rap

RIJKS MUSEUM amsterdam

A New Golden Age

Nicolaes van Gelder (c. 1620-1677), **Still life** (1664).

The *pronk* still lifes from the seventeenth century, with their lavish displays of luxurious foods, can be seen as a symbol of the inconceivable prosperity the Netherlands enjoyed during the Dutch Golden Age. Incidentally, the paintings represent an ideal and do not reflect reality. No one in the seventeenth century, not even the painter himself, ever saw such an opulent array of food displayed all at once, if only because certain of the fruits portrayed ripened in completely different seasons. We can only assume that the chefs, who were usually brought in from France, cooked well, and that the rich therefore ate well.

In subsequent centuries, however, 'thriftiness' became the magic word in Dutch *cuisine*. Good reason, therefore, for the most popular cookbook during the nineteenth century to receive the subtitle: *De volmaakte en zuinige keukenmeid (The perfect and thrifty kitchen maid).*

This frugality continued for quite some time: a possible explanation for the fact that, far into the twentieth century, visitors commonly showed very little appreciation for Dutch cookery. The Portuguese writer J. Rentes de Carvalho who lives in the Netherlands, observed in his book *Waar die andere God woont* (Where the other God lives) published in 1972:

'The Dutch cuisine shows a virtually complete disregard for the joys of the palate. Preferred ingredients are those without taste and smell; seasoning is restricted to salt and a dash of pepper; the dishes are prepared without imagination and almost with con-

tempt. Pea soup, a slice of meat with gravy, porridge, rump steak, applesauce, bread, lots of bread, occasionally a piece of fried fish, bought ready to eat in order to not smell up the house, and, in recent years, an abundance of industrial chicken whose nauseating meat has nothing in common with a real chicken except for the skin — and that's just about it. Add to this some fruit, vegetables and cheese, and I don't think I've forgotten anything, except of course the omnipresent milk in all its guises.'

The Dutch themselves also realized that the time of the extravagant *pronk* still lifes seemed infinitely far away. The popular author Gerard Reve wrote in 1967 that the average Dutch person consumed a little over two litres of wine a year:

'What do you think of that, Bul: more than two litres a year.'

'I wonder where they put it all.'

In the early twenty-first century, this has grown to nearly twenty litres per head of the population. At least we're moving in the right direction.

In 1972, Rentes de Carvalho could only conclude: 'So far, I've only encountered four restaurants in the whole country (I hope there are more), all modest in style, where the food is delicious, the atmosphere pleasant and the prices reasonable.' It is an observation he could no longer make today. Eating is no longer 'reduced to fulfilling a need'. Cooking has become much tastier in and outside the home.

Even though it remains a mystery why a country that, for one and a half centuries, virtually monopolized the world trade in spices has been unable to produce any other culinary legacy than the deep-fried 'doughnut ball', we may nevertheless conclude that the world-renowned French chef Paul Bocuse is quite mistaken when he calls the Netherlands a 'culinary desert'. The Netherlands is definitely in the process of giving shape and substance to the gastronomic riches that can be seen in its seventeenth-century art. Hopefully, this is also reflected in this book.

The Rijksmuseum Cookbook contains ten modern five-course meals created by an equal number of Amsterdam master chefs. These great chefs of different cooking persuasions drew inspiration from paintings representative of the Dutch Golden Age, which can be found at the Rijksmuseum in Amsterdam. The chefs were asked to look at the paintings through the eyes of a cook. The result was surprising: one chef found inspiration for an entire dinner in the pleasant atmosphere of a painting's domestic setting, while

LEFT PAGE *Most seventeenth-century food still lifes, like this painting from 1530, contained an apparent reference to Biblical scenes. When the wine ran out at a wedding feast in Cana, Jesus turned water into wine. One of the guests who sampled the new wine remarked: 'Everyone brings out the choice wine first, and then the cheaper wine after the guests have had too much to drink; but you have saved the best till now.' This comment can be interpreted as follows: if you believe in Jesus, a better life awaits you after this earthly one. Painting by Jan Cornelisz. Vermeyen.*

another chef's recipe had not much more in common with a lavish *pronk* still life than the zest of a lemon. Each chef interpreted the assignment in a very personal way. Although it was not the intention that the meals necessarily had to be prepared in a 'historically correct' manner, one chef immersed himself so deeply in the seventeenth century that he asked us if 'they already had tomatoes in those days'.

Although we had to make the occasional minor adaptation, we also made an effort to retain the chef's own character and cooking method in the recipes. That's why one recipe may be more elaborate than the other. One chef relies entirely on instinct, while the other measures everything to the gram. The recipes are arranged according to restaurant, enabling you to easily prepare the full five-course meal yourself. Naturally, you can also select just one or two of the courses. Or, if you prefer, you can compose your own menu from the fifty recipes provided. The table of contents at the back of the book can help to facilitate this process. Even when the chefs prepared contemporary dishes, we have done our best to place an ingredient or an aspect of each recipe into historical perspective — often in connection with the painting that served as the recipe's inspiration. And if you are a culinarist who reads cookbooks the way a musicologist reads a musical score, you may find your taste buds sufficiently tempted to want to dine at one of the restaurants.

Each menu is accompanied by a short interview with its creator, and each recipe is preceded by an essay on seventeenth-century culinary culture.

The incredible wealth in the Dutch Golden Age led to excesses, such as the tulipomania. Wild speculation on tulip bulbs brought many a person to the brink of ruin. A painting of a tulip was worth only a fraction of a tulip bulb. In order to illustrate in concrete terms the exorbitant price (2,500 florins) paid for one single tulip bulb (a 'Viceroy'), a pamphleteer who opposed the tulip craze compiled a list of items one could have purchased for that amount of money: two cartloads of wheat, four cartloads of rye, four fat oxen, eight fat pigs, twelve fat sheep, two casks of wine, four barrels of beer, two tons of butter, a thousand pounds of cheese, a bed complete with bedding, a suit and a silver goblet. The white with purple tulips in this painting could be Viceroys, the white with red ones might be Semper Augustus, which were twice as expensive. When these tulips were painted in 1639 by Hans Bollongier (c. 1600-1672/1675) they were worth only a fraction of the price paid for them before the Great Commodity Crash of 1637. Incidentally, this floral still life also portrays an ideal, since tulips blossom in the spring and roses in the summer. This means Bollongier never really laid eyes on the bouquet he had painted.

NEXT PAGES *Dirck Hals (1591-1656),* **The Fête Champêtre** *(1627).*

ETATIS·SVE·55·1563 ETATIS·SVE·45
ON HABET
ERGO·MINVS

At the table in the Golden Age

Bread, cheese and beer

In one of his historical pieces, Voltaire (pseudonym of François-Marie Arouet, 1694 - 1778) tells an amusing anecdote about the Golden Age in Holland. Because of his bad digestion ('I was born without a stomach'), the French philosopher was obsessed by food. Perhaps that is why eating customs play a leading role in this story. 'Work and sobriety were their guarantee of freedom. As the Spanish Marquis de Spinola and president Richardot were travelling to The Hague in 1608 to negotiate a cease-fire with the Dutch, they saw along the way a group of eight or ten men disembark from a little boat. The men simply seated themselves in the grass and produced for themselves a packet of bread, cheese and beer. The Spanish ambassador watched, then asked a farmer who these gentlemen might be. They were, the farmer said, the Deputies of the States-General, 'our sovereign lords and masters'. Upon which the Spanish ambassador turned to his companions and said: "Such people cannot be defeated. It is better to make peace with them."' And indeed: the cease-fire agreed upon later was to last for twelve years.

1 In schoolbooks the Golden Age is usually seen as coinciding with the seventeenth century itself. Today, however, historians tend to see it as having begun around 1585, the year in which Maurits (1567-1625), son of the murdered William of Orange (1533-1585), became stadtholder of Holland and Zealand. One year after that, Johan van Oldenbarneveldt (1547-1619) became national counsellor — a function comparable to that of the modern-day Minister of Foreign Affairs. Together, the two men laid the foundation for Holland's glory. Maurits was a brilliant military strategist who fought successfully against the Spanish. Van Oldenbarneveldt was a seasoned diplomat, who saw to a favourable international climate for trade. According to this modern view, the Golden Age also ended around 1672, the so-called 'year of calamity' in which the English, the French and several German bishoprics declared war on the Dutch republic.

The book before you, however, does not deal with such international political developments, and in it the 'Golden Age' (or 'seventeenth century') is taken to mean roughly the period from the end of the sixteenth to the beginning of the eighteenth century.

There is no such thing as seventeenth-century culinary culture. Of course that age did have its own customs and dishes, but although 'the seventeenth century' may sound clear enough, we are, after all, talking about a period of a hundred years in which a country liberated itself from the yoke of Spanish rule and, thanks

During the peace negotiations with Spain held in The Hague, which ultimately led to the Twelve-Year Truce (1609-1621), stadtholder Maurits commissioned the painter Michiel van Miereveld of Delft to paint the portrait of his opponent, Ambrogio Spinola (1569-1630).

LESFT PAGE *Several years before the start of the Eighty Years' War, an unknown artist painted a portrait of the family of the wine merchant Pierre de Moucheron (1508-1567). The family's wealth is reflected in the goods displayed on the table, particularly lavish for that day (detail).*

Was Adriaen van Ostade portraying the average seventeenth-century Dutchman in his **Boerengezelschap** *(Rural Company) from 1661?*

RIGHT PAGE *Or has the average seventeenth-century man been better portrayed by Pieter Codde, with his* **Galant gezelschap** *(Gallant Company) from 1633? (detail)*

to its trading spirit, became the most powerful country in the world. A century in which religious feuds were fought and war was waged. A period in which the population of the Netherlands doubled, due among other things to immigration from neighbouring areas.

With regard to food as well, few sweeping statements can be made because of the vast differences between what various groups ate. It is impossible to say what the 'average seventeenth-century man' was served or placed on his own table. It all depended on whether one shared the modest meal of a small farmer in the countryside, or sat down to a banquet at the urban palace of an Amsterdam regent. And whether that table was set in 1600 or in 1699. The average seventeenth-century Dutchman, therefore, does not exist either.

Petronella Oortman's dollhouse
This beautiful oaken cabinet, decorated with tin and tortoise shell, contains ten furnished rooms (see page 20). The wealthy widow Petronella Oortman (1656-1716) married her second husband Johannes Brandt in 1686. In that same year, a dollhouse was also built for her, and was worked on for the next twenty years by cabinetmakers, painters and other craftsmen. The entire project probably cost somewhere between twenty and thirty thousand guilders. This sum was equal to the price of a house in that day. A real, full-sized canal house, that is.

In one of the rooms of the Oortman dollhouse we find a miniature art cabinet filled with a lovely collection of tiny (real) shells. Some of these shells came from immature specimens, but others were shells from species that never grew any larger.

2 Let's start with a drawer. A drawer that contains something remarkable: a miniature, scale-model cellar. This is the cellar of the 'showpiece' dollhouse of Petronella Oortman, today part of the National Museum's collection. The floor is painted with green and brown tiles. The rear of the cellar is set off with a fence of white wooden planks, complete with a lockable door. Behind this fence, one can see a number of coloured bottles with minuscule corks, and several tiny barrels. Leaning against the fence are a couple of brooms, buckets and a miniature washtub.

The cellar of the dollhouse, in fact, contains several brooms. The cleanliness of the Dutch housewife was proverbial among European travellers. In many travelogues of that day, mention is made of the Dutch love of cleaning. Almost without exception, these travellers praise or mock the spotlessness of Dutch cities and public spaces. According to one of them, who visited Rotterdam in 1699, that cleanliness was born of the fact that the air in Holland was so humid: 'The houses are extraordinary neat withindoors as well as without; and indeed, there is a kind of necessity of being cleaner in this country than in some other places, because of the moisture of the air.'

The Dutch housewife's predilection for order and neatness may also have had something to do with social order in the young republic. Unlike many other European countries of that day, Holland no longer had an extensive royal court or ruling, landed nobility.

LEFT PAGE *The cellar in Petronella Oortman's dollhouse can only be viewed by removing the kitchen floor or opening one of the drawers (see this page on the right side).*

Petronella Oortman's dollhouse

Thanks to the country's burgeoning economy, power was in the hands of normal citizens — people who did not owe their positions to heredity, name or estates. The men earned their money in trade or administration, while the women managed the household; the lady of the house, however, did not scrub the doorstep herself.

Yet cleaning took place most diligently indeed. In our day we might think that people so neat suffered from hosophobia, but all that polishing and scrubbing was done primarily for the benefit of others. Cleanliness served to boost one's status. It was an activity done, not because it was necessary, but for the neighbourhood. 'The neighbourhood' was defined as those who held a social position similar to one's own, and who also lived in a house along the canal. In the Amsterdam of 1650, those houses were usually between twenty and thirty Amsterdam feet (between five-and-a-half and eight-and-a-half meters) in breadth.

In those days, the Dutch word 'schoon' meant both 'clean' and 'beautiful'. Philosophers as early as Plato, after all, knew

Decorative dollhouses

Because no canal-houses have been preserved complete with their original seventeenth-century floor plans and furnishings, dollhouses like these constitutee one of our most important sources of knowledge about what the inside of a house looked like in the Golden Age. These dollhouses were definitely not toys, but were intended as a showpiece for adults.

The predecessors of the Dutch dollhouses were art or curio cabinets: often beautifully ornamented boxes filled with objects which attested to the wealth and good taste of the owner: shells, gems, fossils, animal specimens preserved in spirits. Concealed behind their doors, in their drawers and secret compartments, these art cabinets often contained unknown worlds that were meant not only to show off, but also as an inexhaustible source of entertainment. Cabinets such as these were conversation pieces, displaying not only natural objects but also providing space for manmade objects such as miniatures of silver and other precious metals. It was probably in this way that the Dutch dollhouses developed, almost all of which resembled cabinets when closed, although the German dollhouses of the same period actually resembled a house.

An English traveller to Amsterdam in 1687 described his visit to a cabinetmaker's in the Kalverstraat, where furniture was displayed. He saw a great variety of tables, chests and cabinets. 'To this place every workman in the city must bring his work that is finished

that the beautiful was a manifestation of the good.

The daily cleaning greatly resembled a ritual: the house was the temple of the family, and never before in Western society had the nuclear family been as sacred as during Holland's Golden Age.

Petronella Dunois (1650-1695), as portrayed by Nicolaes Maes.

The popular booklet *De ervarene en verstandige Hollandsche huyshoudster* (The Experienced and Wise Dutch Housekeeper), even though published only in the eighteenth century, provides us with a fine depiction of a seventeenth-century household. A *huyshoudster* was not a cleaning woman, but more like a female butler related to the family by marriage. The booklet contains ten '*zamenspraken*' or dialogues, concerning the running of a household. The second dialogue deals with the organisation of the household and with cleaning. The participants are Christina (the experienced housekeeper)

[...] So that a man sees at once all the choice of things of that kind that are in the whole city.' At the fair in Amsterdam, this same traveller saw a 'wonderful curious rich cabinet' that had been fashioned in the city

of Leiden and was 'twelve years in the making and valued at five thousand pounds sterling.' At that time, five thousand pounds equalled roughly 55,000 guilders. A sum equivalent to approximately 2 million euros in today's terms!

Because these dollhouses employed a great deal of suggestion (there were, for example, often no staircases in them), one might wonder whether the dollhouses actually presented an accurate view of the homes of that day. They would seem more to reflect an ideal world.

The National Museum's collection includes dollhouses that belonged to Petronella Dunois (c. 1676) and Petronella Oortman (c. 1686-1710), as well as the Canal House (c. 1750).

LEFT *The kitchen in Petronella Oortman's dollhouse. The pump in the right rear corner of the kitchen actually worked.*

BELOW *A room in Petronella Dunois' dollhouse*

Petronella Oortman's dollhouse

and her daughters Anna (married) and Maria ('a marriageable maiden'). The young women listen carefully to the words of their mother, whose motto is: 'when all fulfil their duty, then all live in contentment'.

Christina explains to her daughters the tasks of the numerous servants. On Monday, Tuesday, Thursday and Friday, before the lady of the house awakes, the hall, the front house and the doorstep are to be cleaned. And on Wednesday as well. On Saturday one can

All in good time

Some British travellers in the seventeenth century were struck by the differences between British and Dutch clocks. The clocks in Holland not only struck the hour, but also every half hour and every fifteen minutes. A Dutch clock, or a clock made for export to the Netherlands, can also often be recognized by the presence of an alarm. The Dutch lived by the clock, and did everything on time.

According to **De ervarene en verstandige Hollandsche huyshoudster** (The Experienced and Wise Dutch Housekeeper) everything in the household was to have its fixed place and time. Behind this precept we can hear the words of the Preacher from the Biblical book of Ecclesiastes. After the statement: 'To every thing there is a season, and a time to every purpose under the heaven' follows a list of things which determine a man's life: birth and death, sowing and harvest, war and peace. But, the Preacher wonders: 'What profit hath he that worketh in that wherein he laboureth?' In other words: what use is there in working hard when the world goes on without you?

'I have seen,' the Preacher says then, 'the travail, which God hath given to the sons of men to be exercised in it. He hath made every thing beautiful in his time: also he hath set the world in their heart, so that no man can find out the work that God maketh from the beginning to the end. I know that there is no good in them, but for a man to rejoice, and to do good in his life. And also that every man should eat and drink, and enjoy the good of all his labour, it is the gift of God.' We may not know what all our labour is good for, but God knows, so let us do our best and occasionally enjoy ourselves. And that is precisely what the higher social echelons of seventeenth century did: they enjoyed themselves, and allowed others to do their best.

grant the maid a little more time, not to sleep in, but 'in order to clean all with the greatest of care'. On Monday and Thursday afternoons, it is time to do the rooms, on Friday the kitchen and the cellar. Week in, week out. It may, in fact, be seen as something of a wonder that the homes along Amsterdam's canals have not long been scrubbed into to a pulp.

After the meal, the dishes were to be washed immediately. And while the family was at breakfast, beds were stripped and the sheets and blankets folded, care being taken when unfolding them that 'the end of the sheet which had lain at the foot-end is never placed at the head of the bedstead'. Everything was to be fluffed, aired, polished and scrubbed, even the cat litter was filled with clean sand twice a week. But it was also understood that the maid was to have an our or two for herself on Wednesday afternoon, and late in the day on Saturday. In order to mend her own clothes and darn her socks, that is. And she was also to be allowed to attend church at least once every two weeks, but while making sure that she did not sneak off to do other things.

Supplies were to be kept in a secure, locked place. Anna believes that people will talk if you do this, because the servants will think that you suspect them of thievery. Mother Christina isn't bothered by that; she believes the personnel will understand — and besides, as the rest of her discourse demonstrates, she sees that same personnel largely as a light-fingered source of expense.

According to Christina, there are servants who eat so much between times that they become extremely picky during the regular meals. And that is not good; even children must be taught to eat breakfast in the morning, a good supper in the afternoon and not to go to bed with a 'hollow stomach'. All other behaviour, she feels, are 'so many bad customs.' Food is therefore to be locked up tight in the cellar pantry, and regular inventories are to be taken. Christina checks the kitchen and the pantry each morning, to ensure that nothing is being wasted or stolen. One can almost hear the personnel sigh: please leave us alone and go play with your dollhouse. Everything is locked up tight; the natural explanation for why 'Mum' walks around with such a huge key ring. As though, as her brother puts it, she were running an entire orphanage.

'The Alleyway', painted by Johannes Vermeer (1632-1675), has just been scrubbed.

Table clock (c. 1715-1725). This clock played a different melody every hour. The works were made by Andries Vermeulen, one of the best clockmakers in Amsterdam in the early 18th century.

Aᵒ Dnis : 1581
Ætatis suæ 2

The dog as soul mate
In many seventeenth-century paintings we see dogs acting as companions to children and hunters. In church interiors, dogs are often seen as well. For many at that time, the dog was as important as it is for people today. On October 25, 1682, the eighty-six-year-old poet Constantijn Huygens (1596 - 1687), for example, wrote two moving poems about his deceased dog Geckje ('Little Fool'), in which he claimed that there were enough big fools in the world, but only one little fool. The elderly bard would rather have seen that all the big fools died, while his own little fool remained alive.

3 Shopping was done at the market. There were any number of specialised markets where a motley group of vendors (who were held in not particularly high esteem) plied their wares. The markets were scattered throughout the city. Some of them were held on a daily basis, but many less frequently than that. The English heraldic painter Thomas Penson described the various markets he encountered when he visited Amsterdam in 1687: 'The fishmarket, where I bought brave salmon for eight pence the pound; two flesh-halls; the apple market; the flower market; the rag market; the pipe market; the butter market and the dog market, which made me laugh heartily. (...) There I beheld (with great diversion) dogs to be sold of all kinds, from great mastiff to the lady's lap-dog and also cats and young kittens, etc.' This market was held on Monday. Hunting dogs could be bought there. But in those days, dogs were also often used as beasts of burden. An ordinance dating from 1675 shows that the transport of goods by dog cart had become so rampant that Amsterdam placed a ban on the pulling of single- or double-wheeled carts by 'large dogs or hounds'.

But dogs were also well-loved as pets.

Constantijn Huygens, as portrayed by Jan Lievens between 1627 and 1630.

In *The Experienced and Wise Dutch Housekeeper*, Anna explains that her husband feels that a housewife would not have to be as frugal with her things if she did her shopping in bulk: 'should you purchase sugar, rice, etc. in barrels and bales', she could save more

Jacob Willemszoon Delff the Elder (1550-1601), **Portrait of a boy** *(1581) (detail).*

The Kitchenmaid, *attributed to Willem van Odekercken (c. 1610-1677).*

than by checking up on her staff. But Mother Christina says that her son-in-law knows nothing about housekeeping: everyone knows that personnel steal a great deal of the wares. After all, hadn't everyone seen maids who paraded about in clothing they could never afford with their salaries? Then one knew that they were either a 'thief or a harlot'. And their thievery was not limited to the pantry; when sent out for shopping, they cheated you as well: they purloined change, bought an ounce less cheese than you'd asked for, loitered at the 'comestibles market', and on top of that waste their own time 'chattering away' with the bakery maids, and gossiping about everything that takes place in your household. Christina therefore advises her daughters to have the butcher and the baker's boy and the greengrocer's maid come by the house every day to take orders and make deliveries. The ladies will simply have to go the fish market every day themselves, for one never knows what has come in or what the prices are. Anna's husband, fortunately, is 'fond of the buying of fish', and because he must go to town anyway every afternoon, he buys the fish at the market.

But what wares did one find at a market in those days? A painting by Joachim Beuckelaer entitled *De welvoorziene keuken* (The Well-Ordained Kitchen), shows a rich variety of food. It is a horn of plenty that few people in that day would ever have seen, let alone tasted. To the right of the two kitchenmaids we see a huge array of foods, so carefully arranged that it seems as though they knew the painter would be coming along any moment.

We see poultry on hooks: a partridge, a cock, what looks like two snipes and a turkey. More birds and an assortment of small game is lying on platters: a pigeon, a bunch of songbirds, a hare, a rabbit. Further along we see a piece of lamb, and a choice selection of vegetables, such as cauliflower and artichokes, and fruit: grapes, plums and more. One's first impression is that the painter's aim is to show us what he is capable of, but even clearer is that the painter wishes to tell us something; in the background we see a tableau that appears more often in such 'kitchen pieces', which were Beuckelaer's speciality. Through the portal in the distance, we see Christ, visiting the home of Martha and Mary.

Kitchen pieces

Joachim Beuckelaer (1530-1573) painted **De welvoorziene keuken** (The Well-Ordained Kitchen) in 1566. He was apprenticed to his uncle, Pieter Aertsen, but surpassed him in the natural arrangement of a wealth of foodstuffs. **De welvoorziene keuken** is a lavish masterpiece. All in all, it depicts a display of foods which the Saviour would never have considered kosher. The painter has transferred the Bible story 'Jesus visits the house of Mary and Martha' to the sixteenth century. People often claim that painters did this in order to bring religion closer to the experiential world of their contemporaries, but the fact that Beuckelaer would have had no idea what people and houses looked like at the time of Christ must also have played a role.

RIGHT PAGE *Joachim Beuckelaer,* **The Well-Ordained Kitchen** *(1566) (detail).*

The still life

The kitchen pieces painted by Beuckelaer and Aertsen precipitated the popularity of still lifes in the seventeenth century. Not only were the Bible scenes relegated to the background in these paintings, but human figures also faded, to make room for lifeless or, as the poet Constantijn Huygens called them, 'unanimated' objects. The origins of the term 'still life' are not known. But the genre existed even before the seventeenth century.

Even the Ancients painted still lifes. On the walls of Pompeii, buried under volcanic debris in 79 A.D., such still lifes — of, for example, two lemons and a glass of water — can still be seen. During the Middle Ages it fell from favour as a genre in itself, but the depiction of lifeless objects and food in portraits and other paintings did not.

Detail: Martha (with arms spread) en Mary (seated at bottom left) with Jesus.

Before the hearth sits a bedraggled man holding an earthenware jug, which probably contains beer. This was apparently given to him by the two kitchenmaids. One of them is plucking a rooster, the other has just put a chicken on a spit. Later, we will discuss the three men directly behind the maids. All of the figures have their

Martha and Mary

On July 29, 1637, the Dutch Parliament (the 'Staten-Generaal') officially approved a new translation of the Bible. In this 'Parliamentary Translation', roughly contemporary to our own St. James' Bible, we find the story of Mary and Martha as it would have been read in the seventeenth century:

'Now it came to pass, as they went, that he entered into a certain village: and a certain woman named Martha received him into her house.

And she had a sister called Mary, which also sat at Jesus' feet, and heard his word.

But Martha was cumbered about much serving, and came to him, and said, Lord, dost thou not care that my sister hath left me to serve alone? bid her therefore that she help me.

And Jesus answered and said unto her, Martha, Martha, thou art careful and troubled about many things:

But one thing is needful: and Mary hath chosen that good part, which shall not be taken away from her.' (Luke 10:38-42)

Joachim Beuckelaer, **The Well-Ordained Kitchen** *(1566).*

backs turned to the scene with Christ, which is centred horizontally on the canvas, at the height of the golden mean. Christ is seated in the middle, with Mary at his feet and Martha at his side. They are surrounded by several other women.

According to the evangelists Luke and John, Jesus was invited to the home of Mary and Martha in Bethany. Martha prepared a meal and served it to Jesus, while her sister Mary seated herself at his feet and listened to what he was saying. Martha asked Jesus reproachfully whether he failed to notice how busy she was, while her sister did not lift a finger to help. But Jesus replied that, although Martha is worried and distracted by many things, only one thing is important, and Mary had chosen the better part.

It was, incidentally, probably no festive meal that Martha served to Jesus: most likely it consisted of bread, chickpeas or lentils, fish perhaps, and sour wine. Many commentators have talked about this painting, but no one has ever questioned the connection between the kitchenmaids and their lavish display and the house of Martha, which was without servants in the Bible story, and therefore poor.

The Biblical scene framed at the background tells us that, rather than worrying about our fellow man, we would do better to heed the words of Jesus. Unlike our earthly goodness, they can never be taken away from us. This was the choice with which many believers had been faced since the Middle Ages: the choice between a *vita activa* (a life of good deeds) and a *vita passiva* (a life of contemplation).

The figures in the foreground, as we've already mentioned, seem unaware of what is going on behind their backs. They are busy, but without truly being absorbed in their work. The kitchenmaids look quite unhappy, and the luxury that surrounds them is unreachable for simple souls like themselves. But perhaps they will share in the good fortune of Martha, who, at the grave of her brother Lazarus, finally recognised Jesus as the son of God.

But who, then, is the old man with the beard? A young man is leaning with his arm in his lap, and another older man has laid his hand on his shoulder. Unlike the kitchenmaid in the foreground, the old man is wearing no shoes. This could be an allusion to another Bible story; that of Mary and Martha's brother Lazarus, who plays a role in the parable of rich man.

Jesus tells the story of poor Lazarus, begging for a morsel at the gates of a rich man's home. Time and again, he is sent away. Lazarus dies, but in Heaven he is taken into Abraham's bosom. The

Jan Lievens, **The Resurrection of Lazarus**, *(1630-1631). In the middle we see Jesus performing the miracle, and to the left Martha, who seems still unaware that her brother has truly been raised from the dead.*

The Raising of Lazarus

'Now a certain man was sick, named Lazarus, of Bethany, the town of Mary and her sister Martha. (...)

'Then when Jesus came, he found that he had lain in the grave four days already. (...)

Jesus therefore again groaning in himself cometh to the grave. It was a cave, and a stone lay upon it. Jesus said, Take ye away the stone. Martha, the sister of him that was dead, saith unto him, Lord, by this time he stinketh: for he hath been dead four days. Jesus saith unto her, Said I not unto thee, that, if thou wouldest believe, thou shouldest see the glory of God?

Then they took away the stone from the place where the dead was laid. And Jesus lifted up his eyes, and said, Father, I thank thee that thou hast heard me. And I knew that thou hearest me always: but because of the people which stand by I said it, that they may believe that thou hast sent me.And when he thus had spoken, he cried with a loud voice, Lazarus, come forth.

'And he that was dead came forth, bound hand and foot with graveclothes: and his face was bound about with a napkin. Jesus saith unto them, Loose him, and let him go.'

(John 11: 1-44)

Attributed to Pieter Corneliszoon van Rijck (1567-1628), **Kitchen interior with Lazarus and the Rich Man** *(1610-1620). The rich man is sitting at the table and wears a hat; poor Lazarus is lying by the door (detail).*

rich man dies as well, and arrives in Hell, divided from Lazarus and Abraham by an unbridgeable abyss. The rich man appeals to Abraham, but to no avail.

Beuckelaer's scene could be depicting this: the young man at the old man's feet is Lazarus, and the rich man is appealing to Abraham, who does not turn around. The well-stocked kitchen is, of course, extremely appropriate in this context; it is, after all, the kitchen of the rich man who does not wish to share with Lazarus.

In view of the huge number of similar scenes painted by Beuckelaer, Van Aertsen and others, this must have been a very popular

In 1661, Barent Pieterszoon Fabritius (1624-1673) painted scenes from the parable of Lazarus and the rich man. The rich man is sitting at the table while Lazarus is being chased away. To the right, Lazarus is being taken into Abraham's bosom in Heaven (detail).

theme. These paintings were therefore commercial, both in what they depicted and in their message. Kitchen pieces were probably also purchased because people found them attractive, or because they were fashionable.

These paintings depict something of which many people of that day disapproved: sinful excess, there were moderation was considered a virtue. It is hard for us to imagine buying such huge paintings with life-sized depictions of what we condemn. Yet even today, many people watch soap operas 'because they're so bad'. The wealth of food (which returned later in the seventeenth century in the form of decorative still lifes), undoubtedly also exercised a certain fascination. The seventeenth-century patrons who bought a Beuckelaer were not, this writer believes, hypocritical, but felt along with the great French essayist Michel Montaigne (1533-1592) that 'we in ourselves are somehow double, making us not believe what we believe, and unable to extricate ourselves from that which we condemn.'

Lazarus and the Rich Man

'There was a rich man who was dressed in purple and fine linen and lived in luxury every day. At his gate was laid a beggar named Lazarus, covered with sores and longing to eat what fell from the rich man's table. Even the dogs came and licked his sores. The time came when the beggar died and the angels carried him to Abraham's side. The rich man also died and was buried. In hell, where he was in torment, he looked up and saw Abraham far away, with Lazarus by his side.

'So he called to him, 'Father Abraham, have pity on me and send Lazarus to dip the tip of his finger in water and cool my tongue, because I am in agony in this fire.'

'But Abraham replied, 'Son, remember that in your lifetime you received your good things, while Lazarus received bad things, but now he is comforted here and you are in agony. And besides all this, between us and you a great chasm has been fixed, so that those who want to go from here to you cannot, nor can anyone cross over from there to us.'

'He answered, 'Then I beg you, father, send Lazarus to my father's house, for I have five brothers. Let him warn them, so that they will not also come to this place of torment.'

'Abraham replied, 'They have Moses and the Prophets; let them listen to them.'

'No, father Abraham,' he said, 'but if someone from the dead goes to them, they will repent.'

'He said to him, 'If they do not listen to Moses and the Prophets, they will not be convinced even if someone rises from the dead.''

(Luke 16: 19-31)

The cook

During the seventeenth-century, the kitchens of the well-to-do increasingly became the domain of cooks, rather than kitchenmaids. This development was seen all over Europe.
In 1731, therefore, Jonathan Swift (1667-1745) addressed the cook — or, more precisely, the kitchenmaid — in his Directions to Servants. The following fragments are taken from that work.

'Altho' I am not ignorant that it hath been a long Time, since the Custom began among People of Quality to keep Men Cooks, and generally of the French Nation; yet because my Treatise is chiefly calculated for the general Run of Knights, 'Squires and Gentlemen both in Town and Country, I shall therefore apply myself to you, Mrs. Cook as a Woman: However, a great Part of what I intend may serve for either Sex; and your Part naturally follows the former, because the Butler and you are join'd in Interest; your Vails are generally equal, and paid when others are disappointed (...).

'Never send up a Leg of a Fowl at Supper, while there is a Cat or a Dog in the House that can be accused of running away with it: But, if there happen to be neither, you must lay it upon the Rats, or a strange Greyhound (...).

'If a Lump of Soot falls into the Soup, and you cannot conveniently get it out, stir it well in, and it will give the Soup a high French Taste (...).

'Never make use of a Spoon in any thing that you can do with your Hands, for fear of wearing out your Master's Plate.

'When you find that you cannot get Dinner ready at the Time appointed, put the Clock back, and then it may be ready to a Minute (...).

'To save Time and Trouble, cut your Apples and Onions with the same Knife; and well-bred Gentry love the Taste of an Onion in everything they eat.

'Lump three or four Pounds of Butter together with your Hands, then dash it against the Wall just over the Dresser, so as to have it ready to pull by Pieces as you have occasion for it.'

4 There is, at least to our modern eyes, one figure conspicuously absent in Beuckelaer's painting. Amid this well-ordained kitchen, we would expect to find a cook — but in the Low Countries of the sixteenth century, one did not find them at all. Cooking was done by kitchenmaids and servants.

This continued to be the case well into the seventeenth century, although some *burghers* did bring in cooks from France for special occasions. One example is found in the letters of writer and composer Constantijn Huygens (1596-1687), secretary to the House of Orange. In his correspondence, Huygens made extensive mention of the marriage of his daughter Suzanna (1633-1725) to Philip Doublet (1633-1701) on April 20, 1660. A meal, including a great deal of game and meat, was prepared for the 42 guests by the French 'Maistre Jacques', assisted by four other French cooks and five cook's helpers. In an article dealing with this event, Dr. P.J.A.N. Rietbergen says that this French invasion came relatively early, as it was generally only later in the seventeenth century that French cooks began finding employment outside their own country. According to Rietbergen, the four cooks jointly earned some 70 guilders, while the Maistre was 'honoured with a present' of 30 guilders, indicative of the growing 'self-awareness of the master chef'.

A wedding in high society brought huge costs with it. Although it is well known that Huygens could, when he chose, be rather fru-

Pieter Claesz (1597/8-1660), **Still life with turkey pie** *(1627) (detail).*

In this painting by Ferdinand Bol (1616-1680), we see Venus attempting to keep her beloved, the hunter Adonis, from the dangerous hunt. The turtledoves at bottom right symbolize the loving couple. In those days, pairs of doves, pheasants or other wild animals were often given as wedding presents.

gal, money was seemingly no object when it came to his daughter's wedding. He spent no less than 3,544 guilders, 1,200 of which went to bridal clothing in which silk, golden lace and silver passementerie were used. The banquet cost him 879 guilders, 28 guilders of which went to lardon alone. A healthy sum, when we consider that the annual wages of a trained worker in those days were somewhere around 300 guilders. A master carpenter earned 100 guilders more.

No fewer than six hundred candles were used to illuminate Huygen's 'greatest room' during the feast. Rietbergen explains that the dishes served were 'dictated by the wedding presents. It was apparently the custom in that day for people, on occasions such as these, to give gifts 'in kind', in this case in the form of meat or game.' Mary Stuart, Huygens' employer, sent a smoked head of wild boar from England. As secretary to the House of Orange, Huygens had doings with a great many dignitaries, who sent his daughter and future son-in-law all manner of treats: the 'braces of partridge, capons, hares and turkeys' and 'fatted pheasants and lambs' came pouring in. In total '127 parts game & poultry' were served to the 42 guests. In addition, the bills from the butcher and poulterer came to more than 250 guilders in total.

Wedding preparations

On April 1, Constantijn Huygens was already writing letters about the preparations for the marriage of his daughter that would take place only three weeks later. One of these takes the form of a poem sent to the Englishwoman Utricia Ogle (1616-1674), who, after her marriage to Sir William Swann, was to become Lady Swann. Like her sister Trajectina, she was named after the city Utrecht, where she was born when her father — who was married to a Dutchwoman — was serving there as governor. Utricia played harpsichord and lute, and had a lovely singing voice. Huygens referred to her as 'ye charming birdie' ('ghy tooverende vogeltje', which rhymes with the Dutch diminutive form of Utricia's surname: 'Ogeltje') and dedicated his collection of verse **Pathodia** to her. Here below is a portion of the poem 'A MAD. SWANN' (To Madame Swann), written in Huygens' inimitable and comic mishmash of English, Dutch and French:

'This good news I sent to Maertje,
Who doth long after a Taertje
In Palmer her Camer,
Where a keij or a hamer
Shall make us enter,
And lustilie venter
Upon a good Dish
Of flesh or fish,
And, which is to note,
Upon the verie throath
Of our noble Utricia,
Who is no nonicia
In making of a noise
With her excellent Voijce,
To bewitch hearts and eares:
So that a man feares
Almost to sitt neere her.
God bee pleased to steer her
To the Haghe with the first,
To quench our thirst;
For that she must think,
Wee will sing and drink
And fiddle and plaij
As long as we maij
In a short night of Maij,

And as drunken guests
Goe home to our nests,
From whence the next daij
Wee will come and saij,
As is just and right,
Thanks for last night.
Then, Ladij, make hast;
For wee line in a fast
After you and your Roman,
our husband, and no man
Besides them two.
Hier sluyt ick het toe:
Mijn rijmpen is moe,
Moe dichts en moe jocks:
Want mijn Huys is vol Cocks,
Die staen en lardeeren
Voor Vrouwen en Heeren,
Die haer beste kleeren
Vast veghen en keeren,
Om merghen met eeren
Te zijn op een mael
In mijn' grootste Sael,
Près d'un pucelage
Qu'on met hors de page.
Much adoe about nothing:
Want, volgens de noodingh,
L'Ambassadeur de France
Salder mé komen dansse,
Et Monsieur d'Hauteriue
Sal ons oock gerieve
Met sijn' grijse presentie:
Oock met syn' patientie
Den Heer van Bavoy,
Met sijn' Huysvrouw, niet moy
Naerse plagh te wesen.
Verstaet bij desen,
Dit zijn Hollandsche curen,
De naeste geburen,
Wat volck het oock zij,
Gaet men niet verbij
In trouwen noch sterven,
Of men soud 't verkerven.
Adieu, fleur van Vrouwen,
Maeckt geen' Rijmers aen 'tgaen,
Of 'tsal u berouwen.
Eer dit werck was gedaen,
Heb ick ses mael gestaen,
En ses mael gegaen,
En ses mael weer aen
Gestaen en geseten.
Want V. E. moet weten,
Een bruytjen in huys
Maeckt een grouwsaem gedruys.
V. E. kent den Auteur
Le Tres-humble seruiteur.
Haghe the 1 of Apr.'

A glass engraved by the poetess Anna Roemer Visscher (1583-1651), presented as a gift to Constantijn Huygens in 1619.

The L-shaped table was set with a knife, fork and spoon for every guest — a fact Huygens mentions explicitly in his correspondence, and which he therefore considered special. Later we will see that, in Huygens' day, this was very unique indeed.

The guests arrived at three o'clock, and the dinner lasted from four that afternoon to nine o'clock that night. Despite the meal's copious nature, therefore, the guests also had time to catch their breath. Although Huygens held the French guests (including the ambassador) in high esteem, he was delighted when the Dutch guests began the old-fashioned game of '*op sommetjes drinken*'. Rietbergen explains: 'Pairs of table companions hid themselves behind a napkin and took turns alternating between a sip from the other's cup and a kiss, while the other guests drummed loudly on the plates with their silverware.'

Drinking couple *by Jan Havickszoon Steen (1626-1679).*

5 In wealthy seventeenth-century society, it became increasingly common for meals to be eaten in separate dining rooms or fancy kitchens. The cooking itself was done in a kitchen, over an open fire, a facility known as the *snuiver* ('sniffer'). Some of these spaces included a primitive form of cookstove. In order to roast meat, both fresh wares and equipment — a stove, for example — were needed. Most people had to make do with boiling meat that had already been preserved.

Often, there was yet another small room where people ate and carried out all manner of household tasks: the *stove*. These little

Most people slept in box beds, as seen in this painting by Pieter de Hooch (1629-post 1683).

The drawing by Adriaen Pieterszoon van der Venne (1589-1662).

Table and bed

In a drawing by Adriaen Pietersz. van der Venne, probably representing the sleeping chamber of Maurits of Orange in The Hague, we see on the left a four-poster bed that would certainly have befit someone of Maurits' rank.

Another striking element in this drawing is the row of chairs on the left. In the seventeenth century, chairs were always kept with the backs to the wall when not in use. In Maurits' chamber we also see a table. In most houses, a plank was simply laid on a pair of sawhorses when a table was needed.

The kitchen in Petronella Oortman's dollhouse.

After an end was put to the month-long siege of Leiden on October 3, 1574, the Protestant 'Beggars' passed out white bread and herring to the hungry citizens, as can be seen in this painting from that same year by Otto van Veen (c. 1556-1629).

back rooms were used in order to keep other parts of the house as clean as possible. Poorer families not only cooked and ate in the kitchen, but also slept there in box beds. It was the warmest room in the house.

The functional division of rooms did not yet exist in many wealthier homes either. Separate bedrooms began appearing in the seventeenth century, but sleeping in bed rather than a box bed was an unprecedented luxury.

During the Middle Ages, two daily meals were commonly eaten: the first at around eleven in the morning, the last one before bedtime at nine o'clock in the evening. In the course of the seventeenth

Boterham

In **De Schat der Gesondheyt** (The Treasure of Health) from 1636, Johan van Beverwijck, a physician from the town of Dordrecht, advised his readers to smear their butter on bread, because that was the healthiest way to eat this dairy product. Today, most Dutch people still eat 'boterhammen' at breakfast and lunch, a custom that therefore originated in the seventeenth century and which was regarded by many at the

century, this first meal moved closer to the noonhour, and a third meal was added: breakfast.

Breakfast consisted of bread and butter or (grated) cheese. According to the British traveller John Ray, who visited Holland in the summer of 1663, there were five varieties of cheese: the large, round cheeses with a red skin; cumin cheese; green cheese ('said to be so coloured with the juice of sheep's dung'); the occasional camembert-like cheese, and a variety 'like to our common country cheese'. He noted that the green cheese was spread on buttered bread. According to Ray, every Dutch inn had 'hung beef', probably smoked, pickled or dried sides of beef. This, he said, was cut into thin slices and eaten with bread and butter, 'laying the slices on the butter.'

This painting by Willem van Odekercken (c. 1610-c. 1677) shows a maid in the kitchen, scouring a kettle. In the background we see another maid by the fire.

The more exclusive white bread (know as *herenbrood* or 'gentlemen's bread') seen so often in paintings of that day was made from wheat flour, and reserved for the elite. Only a small portion of the wheat itself originated in Holland; most of it came from the area around the Baltic. From the fourteenth century on, this wheat trade with the Baltic laid the foundation for the prosperity of the Golden Age, and was referred to even in the sixteenth century as the *moedernegotie* or 'mother trade'. In order to keep their daily bread on the table, the Dutch waged war twice on the Sont (the narrow seaway giving access to the Baltic) during the seventeenth century. This bread was made to rise, as was the more exclusive variety, by the use of sourdough technique, with the addition of old wine or fermented dough. Yeast did not come into use until the nineteenth century.

time (and sometimes even today) as an aberration. A slice of bread is spread with butter, and then with a thin layer of meat or cheese. A 'boterham' is not the same as a sandwich; a sandwich is a double 'boterham' cut in two, while the 'boterham' comprises a single slice and is open-faced. The word 'boterham' exists only in Dutch, and was therefore left untranslated by James Joyce in his **Finnegans Wake** (1939).

Most of the Dutch ate the less-expensive rye or barley bread. In the mid-sixteenth century, the poorest social echelons ate almost nothing but rye bread: two to three kilos of it a day! Breakfast consisted of porridge or leftovers from the day before. Eating fish at breakfast was also quite common.

On the table beside the mother and her sick child is a porridge bowl with a spoon, in this stirring portrait by Gabriël Metsu from c. 1663-1664.

Bread was often served at warm meals as well, and was probably eaten along with all dishes. A gruel made from bread sometimes formed a side dish. In wealthier society, the more expensive wheat porridge was eaten: a true luxury.

In many households a large pan of meat stew was made once a week, and warmed up at every meal.

Lunch was the main meal of the day, and for many people the only warm one. But poor people in the seventeenth century ate a warm lunch as well, usually a simple stew that stood on the fire for hours, and had as its main ingredients rye, oats, buckwheat, peas (and, later, beans as well) and root crops. Cabbage broth or bread gruel was also served. Like their wealthier contemporaries, at lunch they drank beer or wine, both beverages that were purified and preservable. The water in most Dutch cities of that day was too polluted to drink. Or too salty; during the seventeenth century, the canals of Amsterdam were still brackish with saltwater from the Zuyder Zee that entered them through the River IJ. In the course of the seventeenth century, people began drinking more milk and, outside the cities, more water.

In wealthier circles, the noonday meal consisted of a number of courses. The meal often began with raw or stewed vegetables. Then came the meat dishes, often in the form of pasties. On religious grounds, most Catholics ate fish on Wednesdays, Fridays and Saturdays. The midday meal ended with bread and cheese, sometimes fruit, and in the wealthiest households with something sweet, the taste of the elite.

The ship 'De Hollandse Tuyn' (The Dutch Garden) sails up the River IJ in May 1605, upon its return from Brazil. The water in Amsterdam's canals was connected directly through the IJ to the sea, and was therefore too salty for drinking purposes (detail).

Fresh wares

Seventeenth-century inhabitants, in fact, ate a great deal less meat than people in the Middle Ages. That should come as no surprise when one realizes that the population of Holland doubled from 1 to 2 million in the period 1600-1700. During that same century, Amsterdam grew from a city of 100,000 inhabitants to a metropolis of twice that size. Stock breeding could simply not keep abreast of this demographic explosion. And meat was also not a foodstuff that could easily be brought in from afar. According to Jozien Jobse-van Putten (in her standard work **Eenvoudig maar voedzaam — Cultuurgeschiedenis van de dagelijkse maaltijd in Nederland** (Simple but Nourishing — A Cultural History of the Daily Meal in the Netherlands), the Dutch continued to eat only fresh wares raised in their immediate surroundings until far into the nineteenth century. In those days, therefore, there must have been a great many regional dishes. Transport was too slow to guarantee freshness over longer distances.

Moving goods by canal barge from Haarlem to Amsterdam took three hours; from Amsterdam to Amersfoort took nine, from Rotterdam to Antwerp eighteen hours, from Antwerp to Amsterdam thirty hours.

Spices, sugar and — later — coffee, tea and rice were not perishable, and could therefore be transported over greater distances.

In the late seventeenth century, Jacobus Storck (1641-1692) painted this barge on the River Vecht, close to Nijenrode Castle.

In the painting by Nicolas Maes (1634-1693) often known as *Gebed zonder einde* (Prayer without End) we see an old woman at her prayers. On the table is a piece of salmon, a loaf of bread and two buns, a pitcher — probably containing beer, a plate of soup, stew or porridge, and a dish of butter. The food itself is on the table before her, but at the level of the woman's head we see a niche containing an hourglass, an open book (probably a Bible), a lamp and, hanging on the wall, a bunch of keys: symbols of the passing nature of earthly life and the key to God's eternal kingdom.

On the American web site www.arttoheartweb.com, this painting is recommended as the starting point for a sermon. For a fee, clergymen can download the entire sermon, including a digital illustration of Maes's painting, which they can then project in front of the congregation. According to this sermon, the woman is giving thanks for a simple and humble meal. Yet when we realise that in the Golden Age the truly poor had to make do with rye

For what is this old woman, painted by Nicolas Maes, actually praying?

Cornelis Bisschop (1630-1674), **The apple peeler** (1667) (detail).

6 A recent supermarket survey showed that more than one-half of the meals prepared in Dutch households in the early 21st century still had potatoes as one of the main ingredients. It goes almost without saying that many of those meals comprised either the 'evergreen' Dutch combination of boiled potatoes, boiled vegetables and broiled meat, or mashed potato hotchpotch. One might suppose that the potato has been part of Dutch cooking since time immemorial, but that is not the case. When Vincent van Gogh painted his famous *De aardappeleters* (The Potato-Eaters) in 1885, he was portraying people whose great-grandparents had actually seen the introduction of the potato. First brought to Holland around the year 1600, the potato originally came from the New World. For a time the tuber was popular among the Dutch elite, but soon fell from grace and only returned to favour almost 150 years later. It was not until the mid-nineteenth century that the potato became the most important basic ingredient in Dutch cooking, which it has remained to this day.

Anyone perusing a row of recent best-selling cookbooks, however, will notice that hotchpotches and boiled potatoes are not particularly well-represented. Such dishes can be found in a basic cookbook, but most people have simply learned how to prepare them from a member of their own family (usually their mother). In other words: the list of best-selling cookbooks today seems to barely reflect what actually appears on the table on a daily basis.

Herman Saftleven the Younger (1609-1685), **Fig-cactus in bloom** *(1683).*
The fruits of this cactus are not like 'normal' figs, but nonetheless edible and tasty. Today, they are usually referred to as 'Barbary figs' or 'prickly pear'.

Willem Wegewart the Elder, **mortar in bronze** *(1568).*

The same applies to cookbooks from the past. It is hard to determine just how often the dishes described in them were actually eaten, in part because the writers of these books (like their present-day colleagues) simply copied each other's work and did not dwell on workaday reality, the dishes everyone already knew. A seventeenth-century cookbook does tell us *something* about the dining culture of that age, but *what* it tells us is hard to pinpoint.

Here below you will find a brief overview of the history of the cookbook, up to the eighteenth century.

The first printed publication actually considered a cookbook is *De Honesta Voluptate et Valitudine*, published by Bartolomeo de Sacchi di Piadeno (also known as 'Platina') in Venice in 1474. It is a book about the good life. There had been cookbooks before this one, but they had always taken the form of manuscripts, some of which were copied over and over for centuries. The more than 200 recipes which Platina included in his *De Honesta Voluptate* were taken from a manuscript by Maestro Martino, *Libro de Arte Coquuinaria*, which had been distributed in Italy since approximately 1464 in the form of hand-written copies.

Two lovely peacocks, painted by a man who specialized in poultry and even had his own private menagerie: Melchior d'Hondecoeter (1636-1695).

Mediaeval pie

In her book **Van soeter Cokene** (Of Pleasant Cooking), Johanna Maria van Winter provided a literal translation of one of the Latin recipes from **De Honesta Voluptate et Valitudine**. This was a recipe for date pie (Torte ex Dactulis) with figs, suitable in its simplest form for religious fasts, because it contains no meat, eggs or dairy products:

'Mix well-powdered almonds with fish broth and rosewater, and strain the mixture through a sieve into a dish. Mash together one half pound of pitted dates, a few raisins, four or five figs and three ounces of well-boiled rice in a mortar, and add a bit of shredded parsley, rosemary and goosefoot, which you have first braised in sword-lily oil.

'There is no objection to adding to this livers or tender fish fat. Mash at the same time or separately an ounce of currants, one half pound of sugar, a dash of cinnamon, a bit more ginger and a touch of saffron, and add to the above ingredients. To make it one whole, however, you must add either one-half ounce of flour or roe. This must then be spread in a plate well buttered and covered with dough into which neatly pealed pine-nuts have been stuck.

'As crust for the top you may use crepes if you desire. This pie must bake on a low fire. It is important that it be well-baked. When finished, sprinkle with sugar and rosewater. This is extremely nourishing; it digests slowly; it is good for the liver; it rots the teeth; it augments phlegm.'

The Latin title of the book can best be translated as 'Of True Pleasure and Health'. And in view of the comment about this recipe being bad for one's teeth, we can take that title at its word.

Rembrandt painted these two mysterious **Dead peacocks** *somewhere around 1639.*

Gheraert Vorselman used Platina's book when writing his *Nyeuwen cook boeck* (New Cookbook), which appeared in 1560 but was not the first cookbook in the Dutch language. That was the manuscript from which Vorselman probably took the other half of his recipes: *Een notabel boecxken van cokeryn* (A Notable Booklet of Cooking), first published in Brussels in 1514 by Thomas vander Noot. That book included 175 recipes, presented in rather random fashion. Those recipes included ingredients which seem exotic in our eyes, such as swan and peacock.

One of Rembrandt's more mystifying paintings is *Dode pauwen* (Dead Peacocks). A young girl is looking at two peacocks. One of them is lying on a stone sill, beside a puddle of blood, while the other is hanging by its legs from a doorpost. The presence of the

Peacock

A recipe for peacock or pheasant from **Een notabel boecxken van cokeryen**:

'So shall pheasant and peacock be prepared.

Clean the birds properly and ready them for the spit. And when they are half-cooked, sprinkle them with clove and for two platters with thirty grams of small herbs such as powdered cardamom, clove, black pepper, nutmeg and two ounces of powered cinnamon. Then take a good half litre of rosewater and a half litre of vinegar. Put this on the birds. Collect the spices and put them through a sieve. Add to this mixture one-fourth sugar and half a pound of cinnamon. Take then an onion, and add it to the sugar as you did the other spices. Take the bird from the spit and put it on the platter, and sprinkle it with cinnamon. Add the sauce, that is to say, to the platter, without touching the bird. This sauce tastes nicely with all braised things.'

As you can see, the recipe skips entire steps, and is actually impossible to follow without adaptation. Other recipes explain how one can make sure that the feathers and head of the peacock remain attractive. The bird as a whole could be embalmed, so that it could be used several times to decorate a pasty. Those pasties could also contain meat other than peacock. A different method was to pluck the feathers from head and tail and keep them separate. Around the head and tail of the peacock one then wrapped a cloth, which was kept moist during braising, so that it would later be firm enough to allow the feathers to be replaced.

young girl has caused art historians to speculate about the meaning of this painting.

In art, a peacock in full glory was often chosen as a symbol of haughtiness, pride and false appearance. But, no matter how one tries, it is difficult to attribute those characteristics to these dead birds and the girl. Perhaps a different approach is needed.

Although peacock was commonly served from ancient times up through the Middle Ages — no banquet was, in fact, complete without a peacock — the accounts of the bird's flavour are usually not enthusiastic: the meat was hard and dry. A peacock had to be hung for a long time after being killed. To put it in hunter's terms: only when peacock falls from the hook does it taste as it should.

Because of its dry constitution, peacock meat was considered non-perishable. In addition, popular belief had it that the bird grew new tail feathers each spring. Within Christianity, therefore, the peacock became a symbol of immortality unspoiled by sin, and of the resurrection of Christ. It also does not take too much imagination to see in the hanging peacock the symbol of the cross. Furthermore, the peacock in the painting is hanging on a door, and Christ once said: 'I am the door: if any man enter in, he shall be saved.' The blood on the sill may very well refer to Christ as well, for it is a familiar image in the Bible: '...and the blood of Jesus Christ his Son cleanses us from all sin.' (1 John 1:7). Perhaps that is why Rembrandt has a innocent child behold the peacocks.

St. Augustine's peacock

St. Augustine (354-430) was converted to Christianity under a fig tree. One of the greatest sins he ever committed, in his own view, was the stealing of pears from a tree when he was sixteen. In his **City of God**, he writes about peacock flesh.

'Who else besides God, the Creator of all, could have given the flesh of the dead peacock the quality of being imperishable? When we first heard this, we could barely believe it: yet when served the braised meat of this bird once in Carthage, we had them set aside a piece of its breast, of a size we could choose ourselves. After the course of so many days that any other meat would have perished, that piece was brought forward and presented to us again; it was in no way offensive to the nose. Then it was laid aside again, and after more than thirty days was found to be in exactly the same state. The same was true after one year, excepting that the meaty substance was then dryer and had shrunk.'

And, he added: 'That the flesh of a peacock does not perish, while even that of Plato has perished long ago!'

The most popular cookbook of the seventeenth century was *De verstandighe kock of sorghvuldige huyshoudster* (The Wise Cook or Careful Housekeeper), the first edition of which appeared in 1667, the last in 1802. A longevity illustrated by the comparison of a cook today choosing to still work with recipes written in 1869.

During the second half of the seventeenth century, many cookbooks appeared which had a special focus on healthy living and which detailed the wholesome effects of a variety of new products. These included the cookbook by Cornelis Bontekoe with the formidable title *Gebruik en mis-bruik van de thee, mitsgaders een verhandelinge wegens de deugden en kragten van de tabak. Hier nevens een verhandelinge van de coffee* (The Use and Mis-Use of Tea, Accompanied

A peacock pasty on the table (detail), by Esaias van de Velde (1587-1630).

A coffee plant, in a (detail from a) portrait of the wife of the director-general of Coast of Guinea, by Daniël Vertangen (1600/1601-c. 1684).

In this anonymous painting from around 1500, we see St. Augustine with his heart — burning with faith — in hand. Note the peacock in the background.

Poultry hung to cure, by Willem van Aelst (1626-1683).

by a Treatise on the Virtues and Powers of Tobacco. Including a Discourse on Coffee), from 1686. It was not until 1701 that another truly innovative cookbook appeared: *De Geoeffende en Ervaren Keuken-Meester* (The Practiced and Experienced Kitchen Master). In it, the influence of French taste on Dutch cuisine was already evident. In 1745, a cookbook appeared that was to become even more popular, and which included no fewer than 89 recipes taken from the 'Kitchen Master'. *De Volmaakte Hollandse Keuken-Meid* (The Perfect Dutch Kitchenmaid) remained in print until 1856.

IOHANNIS SAENREDAM
SCVLPTORIS CELEBERRIMI.

Appearances deceive
For example: the seemingly realistic church interiors by Pieter Saenredam are, upon closer examination, more complicated than they seem. If the church still exists, it is often impossible to locate exactly the same vantage point from which the painter worked, because he wilfully moved or removed pillars, adopted a higher perspective than humanly possible, or even painted the interior from a perspective that lay outside the church itself!

7 Following a reading on the subject of phallic symbols, the story goes, one of Sigmund Freud's listeners approached him and asked about the significance of the cigar he had just lit. Freud's purported reply was: 'Sometimes a cigar is just a cigar.'

Those who grew up with René Magritte's *Ceci n'est pas une pipe* might tend to see seventeenth-century paintings as unambiguous depictions of reality. Yet it would be a mistake to do so. *L'art pour l'art* did not yet exist, and, if one thing is clear, it is that a seventeenth-century painting depicted an idealised world.

Floris Claesz. Van Dijck (c. 1575-1651), detail from **Still life with cheeses** *(1615).*

For a long time, no hidden significance was ascribed to still-lifes. In the 1970s, however, art historians began to see them as bearers of a religious or ethical message. Although excesses were not uncommon at first with regard to these interpretations, historians today agree that a still-life may have a hidden significance, but that not every symbol bears the same meaning. Just as Freud noted, the context is what counts.

In the seventeenth-century, the interpretation of paintings was carried out with the help of the emblem books so popular among intellectuals of that day. Emblem books originated in fifteenth-century Italy, when humanists began seeing Egyptian hieroglyphs as symbols for a greater, more profound truth. Although symbols in the Middle Ages were almost always religious in nature, during the Renaissance symbolism took on an increasingly secular signifi-

Pieter Saenredam (1597-1665) completed this painting of the Sint-Odolphus church in Assendelft in 1649. In the right foreground, we see the grave of his father, Jan Saenredam.

NESCIT HABERE MODVM. 91
XLV.

Ovid. 10. Metam. *Nec modus aut requies, nisi mors, reperitur amoris.*
Sen. Oct. Act. 1. *Amor perennis conjugis castæ manet.*
Auson. *Vxor vivamus, quod viximus, & teneamus*
Nomina quæ primo sumpsimus in thalamo;
Neve sit ulla dies ut commutemur in ævo,
Quin tibi sim juvenis, tuque puella mihi: &c.
M 2 Een

An emblem from Jacob Cats' collection of emblemata **Silenus Alcibiadis, sive Proteus** *(1618), with etches made after the style of Adriaen Pietersz. van de Venne, from the collection of the Schuhmacher antiquariat.*

cance. Interpretations were sought in ancient Greek and Roman mythology, and in the work of philosophers such as Plato.

In Holland, the genre took the form of a series of illustrations accompanied by one or more mottoes and a rhyming text. Famous collections of emblamata or '*sinnepoppen*' were those by Jacob Cats and Roemer Visscher.

The emblems themselves, however, are not always as easy to explain as one might suppose at first sight. Under the heading 'From Big to Bigger', Jacob Cats for example shows us a picture of a crocodile straddled by a skeleton. 'He knows no measure' the Latin motto tells us. This would seem to be an exhortation to moderation, but it is not. The emblem harks back to one of Pliny's accounts. Pliny tells us that a crocodile never reaches maturity, and continues to grow all its life 'until its elder years, yea, even into death.' According to Cats, this is the way love should be also: 'True love is that which grows without end.'

RIGHT PAGE *Very thoughtful of the hunter to offer his take to the seamstress, but a great many symbols in this painting indicate that he is interested in more than just staying for dinner: 'vogelen' ('birding'), for example, meant 'making love', and 'naaien' ('sewing') still retains that meaning. Other elements in this painting are also associated with physical love, and the painter Gabriël Metsu (1629-1667) and his contemporaries were unequivocally aware of them all (detail).*

Portrait of Jacob Cats from 1639, by Michiel Janszoon van Miereveld (1567-1641).

Father Cats

The work of 'Father Cats' was immensely popular across all layers of Dutch society. His moralistic poetry was a fixture, alongside the Bible, in the bookcases of countless households. This made Cats a multi-millionaire in his day. In **Waar ligt Poot? Over de dood en de laatste rustplaats van Nederlandse en Vlaamse schrijvers** (Where's Poot Buried? On the Death and Final Resting Places of Dutch and Flemish Writers), we read about his attempts to ensure himself a place in heaven.

'To tip the scales in his favour, in December of 1658 Cats organized a feast for the eight preachers from The Hague who occasionally held services at his home, as well as his two in-house preachers. The chamber was decorated as for a wedding, with Cats' name and age spelled out in a floral arrangement. The meal took place in high spirits. Cats gave all the clerics a copy of his recently published **Tachtigjarige bedenkingen** (Reflections at Eighty) and **Leven** (Life), a mirror and a salt cellar. In return, the gentlemen were to present an ode to the host or recommend him to the Lord. Only one of the ten guests produced an ode; one might guess that this was precisely what Cats had been hoping for.

'He was, in his final years, seized by a bad illness of the kidneys, and after that time took only a little milk at most meals.'

Less than two years later, Cats died, at the age of 82.

Torrentius' mysterious still life.

Moralistic Epicurean

His contemporaries were highly enthusiastic about the meticulously painted still lifes of Johannes Torrentius (1589-1644). Constantijn Huygens believed that Torrentius made use of a camera obscura to give his 'glasses, tins, ceramics and iron objects' an almost translucent quality, in a fashion never seen before then. Yet Huygens had less praise for the way Torrentius lived his life.

Torrentius claimed that he laid a canvas flat before him, and that the painting painted itself. People supposed that this could only be the Devil's work. There were also rumours that he took part in orgies. And he was reported to have said to a number of women: 'My soul desires your body.' These were stories he did not deny, and so when he walked the streets of his home town of Haarlem he was followed by a crowd of admirers.

Art historians are puzzled by how a man who led such a dissolute life could ever have painted an allegory in praise of moderation.

When he was tortured during his trial for godlessness, the only thing Torrentius admitted to was that he had asked people questions such as: 'Who is God?' and 'Where is Hell?' and 'Is the soul immortal?' But he said he never did this with the intention of discrediting the true faith.

Continued on page 56 >

8 Experts estimate that millions of paintings were made in Holland during the seventeenth century. According to some, the total was more than 1.3 million between 1640 and 1659 alone. Inventories drawn up in the homes of wealthy families show that an average household possessed dozens of paintings. And even the homes of those less well-off always contained at least a few panels and canvases.

Probably no more than 1 percent of all art from the Golden Age has been preserved. Of course many 'production-line' paintings have been lost, but we can only assume that a great number of works which we would now consider masterpieces also fell prey to fire, water, insects, vandalism, war and ignorance.

The only surviving work of Johannes Torrentius (1589-1644), for example, was almost lost as well. Torrentius' real name was Jan Simonsz. van der Beeck. His *Still life with pitcher, glass, jug and bridle* from 1614 was discovered in November 1913 by the chairman of the Twentsche Antiquities Association, J.J. van Deinse. He saw the painting at a corner shop in Enschede, owned by a Mr. Sachse. The round panel had apparently been used for years as the lid of a raisin barrel.

This still life is particularly rare because most of Torrentius' work was destroyed after his 1628 prosecution in his home town of Haarlem for loose and godless behaviour. That trial may, in fact, actually have been about Torrentius' leadership of the Dutch

Unique seventeenth century paintings can also be seen on the wall of Petronella Dunois' dollhouse.

Porcelain
It was only in the seventeenth century that people in Holland began collecting crockery in the form of 'services', that is to say: quantities of plates, bowls, etc. decorated with the same motif. This porcelain usually came from China. In his Directions to Servants, Jonathan Swift (1667-1745) wrote:
'When you carry a Parcel of China Plates, if you chance to fall, as it is frequent Misfortune, your Excuse must be, that a Dog ran across you in the Hall; that the Chambermaid accidentally pushed the Door against you; that a Mop stood across the Entry, and tript you up; that your Sleeve stuck against the Key, or Button of the Lock.'

9 Outward appearance — showing off one's riches — was the crux of the matter in the seventeenth century. That becomes clear when we view the fancy kitchen in Petronella Oortman's dollhouse. The enormous china cabinet full of treasures from 'the East' catches the eye. Yet a kitchen like this one was, in those days, not a room where everyone was welcome. This kitchen was the domain of the family and good friends. Today, we would probably call it a 'dining room', and when the German traveller Zacharias Conrad von Uffenbach saw the dollhouse in 1718, that is precisely what he called it: '*die Et- oder Eszkamer*'.

There were no paintings on the wall in Petronella's kitchen, but many such rooms did have them. In the southern Netherlands, in the city of Antwerp, kitchen pieces and still lifes were often found in the kitchen. This was far less common in the north. Family portraits, however, were regularly seen; these portrayals were apparently considered intimate and unsuitable for the parlours located — unlike the kitchen — at the front of the house.

For Dutch *burghers*, eating was something one did with one's loved ones — real or represented. We also know that some Amsterdam merchants had their portraits buried with them, fearing that these works of art would otherwise start to lead a life of their own, distinct from their own personality. And in an eighteenth-century book of etiquette, we read that persons of the 'finest and neatest manners' did not 'seat themselves close to the painting of a person

The 'fancy kitchen' in Petronella Oortman's dollhouse. Most of the crockery is real porcelain, and was made specially for the dollhouse in Japan and China.

A delftware breakfast plate bearing the portrait of Willem III, Prince of Orange (1658).

of high circumstance'.

In Petronella Oortman's fancy kitchen we find no paintings, but a lantern has been skilfully painted on the ceiling, the double window frames are decorated in Oriental fashion, and the impressive china cabinet is filled with porcelain ordered from Japan and China specially for this dollhouse. In addition, we find glass painted to resemble china, and a great deal of glasswork behind the doors of the cabinet.

In the mid-seventeenth century, it was still unusual for all guests at the table to have their own plate, cup and cutlery. Until long after the Middle Ages, it was normal for cups to be shared at the table. Food was served on a slice of bread, later replaced by a small, flat plate of wood or tin. But one cannot conclude from this that meals in the Middle Ages were a crude occasion. The didactic poem

'No likeness at all,' Erasmus himself said about this etching made by Albrecht Dürer (1471-1528) in 1526. With regard to a portrait sketched by Hans Holbein, Erasmus noted: 'O, o, if Erasmus still resembled this, he should marry anon!'

Bouc van Seden (Book of Manners) shows that etiquette did exist, and was quite comparable to what we consider normal: it was well-mannered, for example, to eat at the same pace as one's table companions, not to blow on hot food, and not to put back a piece of food from which one had already taken a bite. In addition, one was not to lean one's elbows on the table or scratch one's head (when others could see it). There were also special rules for women: they were not to become drunken, and they were not to fall asleep at the table.

As with all books of etiquette, of course, it is hard for us to determine how popular they were, and whether people actually acted according to their precepts. Some passages were perhaps even meant to be humorous.

Desiderius Erasmus (c. 1467-1536) wrote a book of etiquette for young people which was republished regularly during the sixteenth century. Erasmus felt that the old or ill, who quickly became tired, should be allowed to rest their elbows on the table. In his *De civilitate morum puerilium libellus* from 1530, he gave young people tips about matters such as how to behave at the table: 'When you are seated, place both hand on the table, not folded and not on your plate. It is impolite to put one or both of your hands in your lap (...). When you rock back and forth in your chair or shift from one buttocks to the other, you create the impression that you are constantly breaking wind, or trying to do so.'

A goblet (called 'Berkenmeier' in Dutch), engraved by Anna Roemer Visscher (1584-1651).

Rum Goblet ('Roemer' from the Dutch, meaning 'to praise', from its use in drinking toasts) engraved by Maria Tesselschade Roemer Visscher (1594-1649).

Erasmus was in Basel when he wrote this book. There forks were already used: 'Place your cup and a clean knife at your right hand, and a chunk of bread on your left. (...) Dipping your fingers in the sauce is boorish. Use either your knife or your fork.' He was, however, still accustomed to sharing a cup: 'Do not raise a cup to your lips without first having wiped them with your napkin or your handkerchief, especially when someone hands you his cup or when you are drinking from a common mug.'

Poultry was placed on the table and carved by the guests themselves. According to Erasmus, it was impolite to take all the nice pieces for yourself.

In his view, one must not become too absorbed in one's food, but should do one's best to listen to the stories told by other, more

The members of a shooting club are seated at the table and being served by an innkeeper and his wife. When Dirck Barendsz (1534-1592) painted his **Fish Eaters** *in 1566, cutlery was apparently not yet a means of achieving social distinction (detail).*

important people than yourself. You should only speak when there is no way around it, or when someone explicitly asks you a question. Then, one should not reply with one's mouth full, for that is impolite. One must also not watch other people eat: 'it is the height of impoliteness to turn your head to see what is going on at another table.'

Criticising what has been set before you is, of course, taboo, and when you yourself are the host 'it is well-mannered to apologise for the paltriness of what is served; but to unduly praise each dish or to mention the price of various ingredients immediately ruins your guests' appetite.'

Being ravenous is bad manners: 'Some people are barely seated before they begin rummaging through the pots with their hands. That is behaviour for wolves.' With striking frequency, Erasmus draws comparisons with animals. Polite people use a knife to scrape the meat from the bone, gnawing is for dogs; licking the plate is for cats; throwing back your head to drink the last drop from the cup makes you look like a stork; people who eat with their

mouths open sound like pigs.

In *De hoofsche welleventheid en loffelijke welgemaniertheid* (Courtly Etiquette and Laudable Manners), published in the early eighteenth century, we see that much of what Erasmus claimed still applied two centuries later. According to that book, stuffing large chunks of food into your cheeks makes you look like a monkey.

The chapter dealing with table manners also grants a great deal of attention to the carving of meat and fish. Many excerpts seem to have been taken from the booklet *De cierlycke voorsnydinge aller tafelgerechten* (The Graceful Carving of All Dishes) from 1664. The strange thing, however, is that the earlier book explains how to use a fork while carving, while in the book published later no mention whatsoever is made of the fork!

In the Middle Ages, the carving of food was a respected skill and part of a knight's training. It was an honour to be asked to do the carving at a banquet. In those days there were many types of knives, including the *presentoir*, a knife which could also be used to dish up food for a lady. The National Museum has two beautifully decorated *presentoirs* from 1532, which came from the court of Charles V. In addition, it was common practice in the Middle Ages for one to bring one's own knife to a banquet.

In the seventeenth century, the rule of thumb applied when carving poultry was to begin with the legs, then move to the wings and finally the carcass. Whereas in our day the custom is to place the animal on the table carved in unrecognisable fashion, at that time the intention was to show the animal in a state as near intact as possible. Fish was served with head and all, also because that was considered the most flavourful. The head of a fish was displayed prominently on the table, and cut in two: 'equally as can be, a sea swine (dolphin or porpoise), a fresh salmon, a carp; and of this latter the tongue being the tastiest part.'

The spine of a pike could best be removed by hand and at the table. First one broke off the tail, then squeezed the back and stomach, after which the head could be removed along with the spine, which was 'laid with a flourish on a special table plate.' The head was then separated from the spine and placed back with the fish.

There were also other animals that tolerated no cutlery. 'Many

The fork
It is not clearly exactly when the fork entered general use in the Netherlands, but in his enlightened broadsheet **De Hollandsche Spectator** in 1733, Justus van Effen wondered aloud: 'When one dines with clean and honest fellows, I do not find the use of fingers and the sharing of the cup to give the slightest reason for offence. What is to keep hands, that have been properly cleaned, from being as pure as a scoured or washed fork?'

Apparently, for someone who had never used a fork, learning to use one was as difficult as the prospect of not using one would be for us. Table manners are, after all, not devised to make eating easier, more hygienic or healthier, but to stand out — etiquette is a means of distinction. Violating etiquette is as well.

Jesus breaking bread through the centuries. From top to bottom, three details from **The Last Supper**: *The Passion of Roermond, c. 1435; Jacob Corneliszoon van Oostsanen, c. 1525; Gerbrandt van den Eeckhout, 1664.*

Two rabbits, complete with 'trotters'; detail from a still life by Cornelis Lelienbergh (d. 1676).

wish to have no knife applied to a roasted hare, but pinch between the right thumb and fingers small pieces of flesh from back and ribs, then breaking off the head and legs.' One also displayed skill at the table by 'wringing away' the head and limbs of a roasted rabbit. And if you then arranged the pieces in a neat and orderly fashion, your reputation was assured: 'it is a thing graceful to behold'.

Nuts and fruit were eaten directly from the plate, while fresh fruit was to be served without the skin, 'though in this age at many places it is served without the effort of peeling it.'

It was also considered extremely rude to refuse food, especially if one went on to explain why: 'I cannot eat this, I cannot eat that, I never eat roast, I never eat lamprey; I can eat nothing peppered, or with nutmeg & onion, etc.' The writer of this book considers this to be 'bumptious aversion' and easily overcome. Once must simply accept all that is offered, and if one has a congenital 'insuperable distaste', one may simply leave the food on one's plate and then 'when no eye beholds it' have it removed by a servant.

Some rules are all too familiar to us: it is bad manners, for example, to reach across a plate to take something else. On the other hand, foreign to us is the statement that one may use the same spoon with which one has eaten to dish up more food, as long as one wipes it first with a napkin. Yet even in those days some people shuddered at the thought, and some dishes were served 'with spoons in them which serve no other purpose than to ladle the sauce.'

In our eyes, it is also peculiar to see that people in the seventeenth century kept their hats on during a meal, something which in our day is considered extremely impolite. When one is invited to a meal, one must wait until assigned a seat, and then hold one's hat in hand until the more important people have put theirs back on. If you then wish to offer someone a plate or platter, it is polite to take off your hat the first time you do so, but not after that 'so as not to confuse or confound'. If someone of higher rank offers you a plate, you must accept while doffing your hat.

Doffing your hat in the proper fashion was something you learned at an early age, as we see in this painting by François Verwilt (c. 1623-1691).

This custom is illustrated in a lovely painting by Bartholomeus van der Helst (1613-1670), which shows the Amsterdam *Schutters-*

Genius or not

Van der Helst's painting of the Amsterdam Schuttersgilde (Shooting Club) at its banquet in honour of the Treaty of Munster is a masterpiece which was, until the mid-nineteenth century, often held in higher esteem than the 'Night Watch'. Unlike Rembrandt, in this gigantic painting from 1639 Van der Helst made use of a huge palette of colors and even lighting. The fact that in the nineteenth century Rembrandt gradually came to be considered more important than Van der Helst probably has to do, among other things, with the appreciation so characteristic of that day for ingenious painters with a personal style and a turbulent life.

In the influential — and, due to its panoramic perspective, still impressive — **Het land van Rembrandt** (The Land of Rembrandt), written in the period 1882 - 1884 by the nineteenth-century critic and essayist Conrad Busken Huet (1826 - 1886), Rembrandt is presented as a superhuman genius who raised everything he painted to a higher level, and whose shortcomings we can therefore only forgive: 'Rembrandt's Anatomy Lesson, his Night Watch, are poems (...). Normal people and normal things he saw in an unusual

way. (...) He made of them supranatural beings. More than the women, the gambling or the wine, he loved his profession and thrived in it. Despite his grey whiskers and greying pate, his portrait from 1660 shows a lively man. (...) The experts discern different periods in his career, all marked by the same power. Only death kept him from producing into eternity. (...) He elicits such confidence that, even when we do not understand him, we convinced of his correctness. Should it have been otherwise, we think, then he would have done so, for he could do anything.'

Rembrandt as God. In the final sections of his study, Busken Huet says that Rembrandt even looked like a man of wonders. 'And, at the head [of the Dutch school painting — ed.] Rembrandt cut a fine figure (...) with his candid face, his beret over one ear, the cloak around his shoulders, a distinguished appearance. He was the handsomest Hollander who ever lived.'

Busken Huet even saw Rembrandt's style as a guideline for the working methods of the historian, and agrees with the pronouncement made in **Physics and Politics** (1872) by the British historian Walter Bagehot (1826-1877): 'The best history is but like the art of Rembrandt; it casts vivid light on certain selected causes, on those which were best and greatest; it leaves all the rest in the shadow and unseen. To make a single notion illustrate a principle, you must exaggerate and you must omit much.' And that is exactly how Busken Huet wrote history.

gilde (Shooting Club) at a banquet in honour of the Treaty of Munster. One of the men is serving another a pasty. The recipient is holding up his plate and has removed his hat. We can also see that not all the guests have their own plate, glass and cutlery. On the left we see a man using the tip of a knife to bring a piece of meat to his mouth. The man dishing up the pasty seems to be using a fork. The fork gradually came into use during the sixteenth century. Originating in Italy, where it had common for some time, the fork came to the Netherlands by way of France. Before that, it was used only at the royal court by those charged with carving meat.

In the seventeenth century, keeping your hat on at the table was not impolite, as long as you took it off at the right moment.

'The handsomest Hollander who ever lived'? **Self-portrait** *of Rembrandt van Rijn (1606-1669)* **as the Apostle Paul**.

10

Although the name is based on matters which barely play a role in the context of this publication, it is perhaps good to stop and consider why the seventeenth century in the Netherlands is referred to as the 'Golden Age'. The term was probably coined only in the nineteenth century, at a time when Europe as we now know it was formed under the influence of a variety of nationalistic movements. While Germany and Italy were being formed, the Austro-Hungarian and Ottoman empires were disintegrating. France and England were confirming their status as world leaders. In the nineteenth century, the Dutch took as their example the nation's flowering: the period in which the Republic possessed a hegemony on world trade and was the most powerful country on earth. The seventeenth century was golden, and Rembrandt was a national hero.

A century of 'spirit and fantasy': Rembrandt Harmenszoon van Rijn (1606-1669), **Faust**.

In his 'sketch' *Nederland's beschaving in de zeventiende eeuw* (The Culture of the Netherlands in the Seventeenth Century), the historian Johan Huizinga (1872-1945) rightly notes that the name 'Golden Age' is inaccurate, and that it smacks of the 'land of Cocagne' spoken of by Ovid in his *Metamorphoses*. 'If our flowering is to have a name,' Huizinga continues, referring to all the work carried out in that age in any number of areas, 'then let is be of wood and steel, pitch and tar, paint and ink, daring and piety, mind and fantasy.'

Although his view is a miracle of nuance compared with the uncritical adulation of the nineteenth century, Huizinga's account

This silver dish from 1613 by Paulus van Vianen (c.1570-1613) shows another scene from Ovid's Metamorphoses, *namely the story of Diana and Actæon. The shepherd Actæon caught a glimpse of Diana, goddess of the hunt, while she was bathing. To punish him, she turned him into a stag, and he was torn to pieces by his own dogs.*

Allegory for the flourishing of Dutch fishing after the Second English Naval War (1665-1667). Dutch naval heroes like De Ruyter, Tromp and Evertsen pull in the nets (attributed to Willem Eversdijck).

RIGHT PAGE *Johann Friedrich Grüber,* **Still life** *(c. 1662-1681) (detail).*

NEXT PAGES *Brothel scene, painted in 1650 by Nicolaus Knüpfer (1603-1655). Born in Leipzig, Knüpfer moved to Utrecht in 1630.*

is also dominated by admiration for all which the seventeenth century had produced. That his book was written and published during the darkest days of the Second World War certainly played a role in this.

'Golden' is a description which can no longer be separated from an age which gave the world some of the greatest painters of all time. Yet a survey carried out by the National Museum recently showed that, today, more than sixty percent of all Dutch people did not know to which century the Golden Age referred.

Is that lamentable? Those who do know are probably not better, richer or happier than those who do not. A knowledge of history, however, may very well help us to determine our perspective on the world and our own situation. Furthermore, as Seneca once wrote, it is 'better to know useless things than to know nothing at all.'

History begins where memories end.

Golden Age

The term 'Golden Age' comes from classical antiquity. In the first book of his **Metamorphoses**, Ovid (43 B.C.-17 A.D.) divided history into ages, and (in the famous translation by the English poet John Dryden, a contemporary of the seventeenth-century Dutch poet and Ovid translator Joost van Vondel) he began with:

'The golden age was first; when Man yet new,
No rule but uncorrupted reason knew
(...)
The flow'rs unsown, in fields and meadows reign'd:
And Western winds immortal spring maintain'd.
In following years, the bearded corn ensu'd
From Earth unask'd, nor was that Earth renew'd.
From veins of vallies, milk and nectar broke;
And honey sweating through the pores of oak.

Adriaan van Raab van Canstein:

'I cook what I would like to eat myself.'

Restaurant Le Hollandais

Amsteldijk 41

1074 HV Amsterdam

T 020 679 12 48

lehollandais@planet.nl

www.lehollandais.nl

Adriaan van Raab van Canstein: 'I started Le Hollandais eight years ago. Four years later, my partner quit because he found the restaurant too small and there was no room here to expand. My view is: it has to remain fun. I have a restaurant because I love to cook.

'We have two cooks and an apprentice. That's a lot of hard work, but when you're in the kitchen yourself five days a week, of course, you maintain good feeling with all the dishes. I draw my inspiration from the refrigerator. You stand there staring a little blankly into the fridge, and then suddenly you know what you're going to make. I cook what I would like to eat myself.

'A good cook is interested in leftovers. When you come into the kitchen and you feel like making something, you're already moving in the right direction. When you walk down a street market, or even through the supermarket. A good cook also likes to keep on eating. He doesn't have to be fat, but he has to be a good eater. Of course you have to have a sound background. And someone who taught you a love of cooking. That can be a professional teacher, but it can also be your grandmother, who once let you help her bake a wonderful pie.

'I don't do much cooking at home, I'm usually at work around dinner time. At home I'm often too lazy to cook. It starts with the fact that I don't feel like washing dishes. That laziness comes from here, because the restaurant has someone who washes the dishes.

Adriaan van Raab van Canstein

When I'm not working, I can draw great enjoyment from a Surinamese takeaway or French fries.

'It was difficult for me to put the recipes for this book down on paper. I tend to cook by instinct. When you make a terrine, for example, you don't weigh all the ingredients down to the last gram.

'People say I cook simply, honestly and purely. No la-di-da. A wee bit conservatively. That's the French influence. I became familiar with French rural cuisine back when I lived in the countryside of Lot-et-Garonne, a fairly desolate part of the Gascogne. I cooked for the local guests in an old, ramshackle hotel. A fifty-franc menu. A hefty meal: garlic, onion, green cabbage, goose lard, a chunk of pork and a bay leaf. That's it. And then you just go on trying to perfect that. That's my ambition. That's what I like most.'

Pheasant terrine

and a salad with cep mushrooms

ingredients for 4 servings

for the terrine

1 pheasant

500 g/17.5 oz (free-range) pork belly, coarsely ground

100 g/3.5 oz lard, thinly sliced

2 slices of stale white bread

50 g/1.75 oz butter

2 dl/7 fl oz white wine

3 cloves garlic

1 onion

1 bay leaf

for the salad

a choice of green lettuce leaves

200 g/7 oz cep mushrooms

1 clove garlic

parsley

butter

In the seventeenth century, a magnificently presented peacock or turkey pie was frequently the showpiece of a banquet. What follows is a festive starter that will taste even better if you let it 'ripen' in the fridge for a few days.

The terrine Brown the pheasant lightly in the butter until golden. Add the chopped onion, garlic, white wine and bay leaf. Braise for 1 hour until done, leaving the lid on the pan. Remove the meat from the bird's carcass and reserve. Cut the crust off the bread and heat the bread in the pan drippings. Stir the mixture with a whisk until it resembles a thick pulp. Let it cool, then combine all of the meat with this panada. Season the mixture with salt and pepper. Line a (2.25 pt) terrine tin with the lard. Fill the tin with the meat mixture and press down firmly. Close it up with the overlapping lard slices and cover with aluminium foil. Bake the terrine in a moderately hot oven (180°C/350°F) for about 1 hour, or until done. Let the terrine cool, and apply some pressure by weighing it down with a heavy object, but make sure that the juices do not overflow. The terrine should preferably 'ripen' in the fridge for several days.

The cep mushrooms Slice the cep mushrooms and sauté them in a little butter until golden brown.

Bartholomeus van der Helst (1613-1670), **The Celebration of the Peace of Münster, 18 June 1648 in the Headquarters of the Crossbowman's Civi** *(c. 1649).*

No other bird has gained popularity as rapidly as the turkey. That is still reflected today in its various names; after all, didn't Columbus think that he had landed in India? The Dutch word 'kalkoen' is supposedly derived from Calcutta, and the English name 'turkey' also hints at a bird from the East, as does the French name 'dinde' or 'dindon', in which we can still hear 'd'Inde' (from India). Fifty to a hundred years after its discovery in North America, the turkey could be found on tables throughout Europe. Before long, it had driven the less tasty peacock from the menu. Like the pheasant in this recipe, the turkey only served as one of the ingredients in the seventeenth century. By the way, the mixture was usually scooped from the rock-hard crust. As can be read in De Volmaakte Hollandsche keuken-meid *(The perfect Dutch kitchen maid): 'This crust is rarely or never eaten', but it's re-used just like the stuffed bird on top.*

The presentation Serve the slices of terrine at room temperature with a fresh salad and the sautéed, sliced cep mushrooms, topped with garlic and parsley.

Oyster and lovage soup

Pieter Claesz (1597/8 - 1660), **Still life with turkey pie** *(1627).*

Salt was precious in earlier times. It came from far away, and its extraction was a time-consuming endeavour. The Dutch traded extensively in this commodity. In the fifteenth century, their salt ships were frequently ambushed and raided by the English. In the sixteenth century, the Dutch started to extract salt on the Cape Verdean islands and in the Caribbean area. In the early seventeenth century, Holland was responsible for 90 per cent of the salt exports to the Baltic Sea region. Salt was thought to have all sorts of remarkable properties: not only was it healthy, but salt could also be used to predict the future and drive away witches. But, most important of all: salt was able to improve the taste of food, as the then immensely popular poet and moralist Jacob Cats wrote: 'Everything that feeds mankind is no good without either salt or brine.'

From time immemorial, oysters have been considered an aphrodisiac. No wonder they constituted a regular item on the menu of the greatest seducer of women in history, Giacomo Casanova (1725-1798). His recipe for seduction went as follows: take two innocent girls, some lemon, a bottle of rum, sugar, hot water and a bottle of champagne. Prepare a bowl of good punch. Then you order two times fifty oysters. Give the girls the punch. And then, in the words of the master himself (as quoted in Casanova à la carte by Ruth Bombosch): 'After we had eaten five or six oysters (...) I had the idea of asking Emilie to slide an oyster into my mouth with her lips. "Of course, you're far too intelligent," I added, "to suspect something behind this."'

ingredients for 4 servings

- 24 Zeeland creuse oysters No. 2
- 1 litre/36 fl oz light chicken bouillon
- 2 sprigs lovage
- 1 clove garlic
- 40 g/1.5 oz butter
- 40 g/1.5 oz flour
- 1 lemon
- croûtons

We are accustomed to eating oysters either raw or grilled, but this soup demonstrates the variety of ways this shellfish can be used. To open the oysters, use an oyster knife with a sturdy, stainless steel blade. Insert the knife into the hinged part of the shell. Then gently twist the length of the blade, prying the shells apart. Cut the adductor muscle on the top part of the shell and loosen the oyster.

Remove the oysters from the shell and set them aside. Add the oyster liquor to the chicken bouillon. Bring the soup to the boil and carefully skim off any foam. Put the garlic through a garlic press and add to the soup. In a small bowl, knead the flour into the soft butter. Thicken the soup with this 'beurre manie'. Season with very finely chopped lovage, salt, pepper and lemon juice. Add the oysters, sprinkle with croûtons and serve immediately.

Braised pork neck ('procureur roast')

with chicory hotchpotch and stewed shallots

Jan Victors (1619-c. 1676), **The pork butcher** *(1648).*

In the seventeenth century, many people in rural areas (but also city dwellers) used to buy a pig in the autumn and slaughter it in November, the slaughtering month. The meat was pickled, dried or smoked, and it was ground and made into sausages. Everything was used -from trotters to head and from brain to blood. This made it possible for people to enjoy meat from time to time throughout the winter — even if it wasn't fresh. The more affluent people bought fresh meat at the market. In Victors' painting on the right we see children making a balloon from a pig's bladder.

All of a pig's meat is edible – you can verify that at any French pork butcher ('charcutier'). In old Dutch cookbooks we also find elaborate guidelines explaining 'How to cut up a pig' and 'How to deal with it, and make the best use of everything'. This dish calls for a cut of meat from the animal's neck, called 'procureur' in Dutch. It can be purchased at any good (free-range meat) butcher.

The 'procureur roast' Brown the pork neck lightly in butter and deglace with the white wine. Add the peeled shallots and braise everything for about 45 minutes or until tender.

The hotchpotch Boil the potatoes in their jackets for about 15 minutes until done. Peel the potatoes and return them to the pan. Mash the potatoes with butter and as much cream as necessary to obtain a fluffy consistency. Cut the chicory into very thin slices and add to the mashed potatoes. Stir well and reheat if necessary. Season with pepper and salt. Serve the hotchpotch with the sliced pork, gravy and shallots.

ingredients for 4 servings

for the 'procureur roast'

500 g/17.5 oz (free-range) pork neck

500 g/17.5 oz shallots

white wine

butter

for the hotchpotch

500 g/17.5 oz potatoes, boiled in their jackets

4 heads chicory

butter

whipping cream

pepper

salt

Granité of grapes

with crème fraîche

Ary de Vois (1630/1635-1680), **Young woman with a parrot** *(1660-1680).*

Grapes have been used since the Middle Ages as an acidic agent (unless people had enough money to buy lemons or vinegar). The juice of sour, unripe grapes is called 'verjuice', named after the French for 'green juice': 'vert jus'. Verjuice was alternatively made of green apples, gooseberries or other sour, seasonal fruit. The taste is not as sharp as that of vinegar. Special grapes were grown for verjuice.

'Granité' is the French name for the Southern Italian 'granita': water ice flavoured, for example, with fruit juice or coffee and sugar. Wine is also commonly used in its preparation. Granité has a grainy structure because the water and sugar crystals are not frozen together. This type of water ice is of Arabic origin. It was consumed between courses to clear the palate.

ingredients for 4 servings

for the granité

500 g/17.5 oz white grapes

100 g/3.5 oz sugar

2 dl/7 fl oz white wine

for the crème fraîche

100 g/3.5 oz crème fraîche

4 gingersnaps

The granité Slowly cook the washed grapes and the sugar in a covered saucepan. Purée the mixture (with a hand blender) and strain. Stir in the white wine. Transfer to a flat dish, preferably of stainless steel. Place the dish in the freezer and stir with a whisk every hour until the mixture is frozen (about 4 times).

The crème fraîche Beat the cream with a little sugar until stiff.

The presentation Serve the granité on ice-cold plates, together with the cream and a gingersnap.

Charlotte of apple, vanilla and lemon

Floris Claesz. van Dijck (c. 1575-1651), ***Still life with cheeses*** *(1615).*

In the Middle Ages, eating apples (and fruit in general) was not considered healthy. That was probably attributable to Adam and Eve having eaten the forbidden fruit of the Tree of Knowledge, thus committing the first sin. Actually, nowhere in the Bible does it say that the fruit was an apple. It was most likely a fig, which explains the fig leaves that were needed after the fruit was consumed. In the seventeenth century, fruit was often eaten for breakfast. That's why a painting, such as this one by Van Dijck, was called a 'breakfast piece'.

A 'charlotte' is a pudding made in a dish lined with ladyfingers or bread. Back in the eighteenth century, a recipe for 'Apple Charlotte' was published in England. In 1854, it was proclaimed: 'A good pudding for those who can not eat pastry.' The name was supposedly derived from the wife of King George III of England.

ingredients for 4 servings

4 sweet apples

100 g/3.5 oz butter

100 g/3.5 oz sugar

1 vanilla pod

grated zest of 0.5 lemon

8 slices of stale white bread

butter and sugar

Peel, quarter and core the apples. Then cut each quarter in half. Remove the crust of the bread and cut each slice into four squares. Place them on a large plate. Melt the butter and sugar in a non-stick frying pan. Spread half of the mixture over the bread. Let the rest caramelize lightly in the pan and add the apples, lemon juice and vanilla seeds. Simmer at medium-high heat until most of the liquid has evaporated and the apples are cooked. Line four ramekins (small round ovenproof bowls with a straight edge) with the pieces of bread, sugared side facing the walls of the bowl and overlapping. Press down firmly. Finish by placing a piece of bread on the bottom. Distribute the apples over the bowls, push down again firmly and cover with aluminium foil. Bake for 30 minutes in a hot oven (250°C/482°F). The bread has to look golden brown on the sides. Unmould the charlottes and top them with a pat of butter. Sprinkle with sugar and serve.

Oysters with smoked salmon and cucumber

Willem Claesz. Heda (1594-c. 1680), **Still life with gilt cup** (1635).

The rolled-up almanac contains pepper. In the seventeenth century, the almanac was an indispensable household aid for the well-to-do middle classes. Dozens of different editions were published every year. The Enkhuizer almanak (Enkhuizen Almanac) was founded in the late sixteenth century and is still in existence today. However, the oldest edition preserved is a fragment dating from 1596, which was found in the Behouden Huys (The Safe House) on Nova Zembla and is now exhibited in the Rijksmuseum. Almanacs contained a calendar, information about tides, sunrises and sunsets, but also the schedules of tow barges, and the prices of merchandise. The almanacs were printed in large numbers, but very few have been preserved, because the pages ended up serving as tubes for tobacco and spices, or for a more lowly purpose.

It is said that oysters should preferably be eaten in months with an 'R'. That's when oysters are supposed to taste better and are less likely to spoil because they're harvested from cold water. This custom actually has its origin in overfishing, which occurred in the seventeenth and eighteenth centuries. In a good year, French fishermen brought 10,000 to 20,000 tons (22,400,000 lb - 44,800,000 lb) of oysters ashore, with the result that the oyster banks in the North Sea became depleted. King Louis XV therefore decreed in 1759 that oysters were not to be harvested and sold between 1 April and 30 October.

ingredients for 4 servings

16 flat oysters
1 cucumber, cut into thin julienne
2 slices smoked salmon, cut into thin julienne
2 shallots, finely diced
8 sprigs dill, finely chopped
3.75 dl/13.25 fl oz crème fraîche
lemon juice
salt and pepper to taste

Cut the cucumber and salmon into julienne strips and combine them in a bowl with the shallots and dill. Mix gently. Add just enough crème fraîche to obtain a creamy mixture. Season with pepper and salt. Add a little lemon juice, if desired.

Open the oysters and clean both the oysters and the deep halves of the shells. Place the shells on a plate that is covered with crushed ice or seaweed. Fill the shells with the creamy salmon-cucumber mixture, top with an oyster and serve.

Warm confit of pork belly

with apple and chicory salad

ingredients for 4 servings

for the pork belly

900 g/2 lb pork belly (cut in quarters)

60 g/2 oz coarse sea salt

1 kg/2 lb 3.33 oz lard or goose fat, melted

for the salad

4 heads chicory (Belgian endive)

3 apples (Granny Smith)

4 sprigs parsley, chopped

1 dl/3.5 fl oz olive oil

juice of 1 lemon

10 g/1 tbsp Dijon mustard

20 g/2 tbsp caster sugar

salt and pepper

Pork belly is a much-used ingredient in many kitchens of the world. For instance, it is used to make the Indonesian babi pangang *(spicy Indonesian pork). And the Italian sausage* pancetta *is pickled, rolled up pork belly. Even the popular Dutch* speklapjes *(thick slices of bacon) and* zuurkoolspek *(streaky bacon) are pork belly cuts.*

The pork belly Quarter the pork belly and score the squares diagonally on both sides. Salt well. Place the pork belly squares in a dish fat side down and leave in the fridge for 24 hours. Then rinse off the salt and dry thoroughly. This procedure ensures that nearly all the water is drawn from the belly and that the skin gets nice and crisp during roasting. Preheat the oven to 150°C/302°F. Place the squares in an ovenproof dish and cover them with melted lard or goose fat. Cover the dish with a lid and cook in the oven for 1.5 to 2 hours until the meat is very tender. Remove from the oven and leave to cool in the fat. Then transfer the squares to a clean dish and cover again with melted fat. Before serving, transfer the squares from the fat to a baking tray and place them in the oven preheated to 200°C/392°F for 8 to 11 minutes, until nice and crisp. Check to ensure that the meat does not brown too quickly!

The salad Cut the chicory in half lengthwise, remove the core and cut into julienne strips. Quarter and core the apples, and cut into fine julienne strips. Combine the mustard and sugar in a bowl and,

David Teniers the Younger (1610-1690), **Country Fair** *(c. 1640-1660).*

The country fair was an annual highlight in the lives of many seventeenth-century people. Here we see peasants enjoying themselves to the hilt. One of the men is sprawled on the ground among the pigs. Everyone is busy eating, drinking, discussing crops or making music, but the occasion was also used to place petty criminals in the pillory or to publicly humiliate malfeasants. The peasants indulged in smoked eel, herring and all sorts of sweets. Festivities were equally popular in the upper classes. The elite often appeared in masks, under the motto: everything is allowed as long as it's done discreetly. When Stadholder William III, who after his marriage to Maria Stuart became king of England, was in London during the time the world-renowned The Hague Fair was held (on 10 May 1689), he said with a deep sigh that he would be willing to give 200,000 guilders if he could fly like a bird across the North Sea to The Hague.

little by little, add first the lemon juice and then the olive oil. Stir together well and correct the seasoning. Mix the dressing with the apples, chicory and chopped parsley. Place a quarter of this salad in the centre of each plate and top with the confit of pork belly.

Soufflé Suissesse

Rembrandt Harmensz. van Rijn (1606-1669), **Tobit and Anna with a kid** *(1626).*

In this apocryphal biblical setting we see a cosy fire, as was usually found in most seventeenth-century households. There was a fireplace in a corner of the kitchen with a tripod from which a pot was suspended. In De verstandighe kock *(The sensible cook) (1669) the reader is offered directions for making a 'serviceable stove'. It concerns a brick structure with an iron door, closed on top, except for a round hole on which a pan can be placed. 'Some people with large households can make the dimensions of the stove so large that four or more pots or casseroles can cook or simmer on it simultaneously.'*

ingredients for 4 servings

45 g/1.5 oz butter
45 g/1.5 oz flour
5 dl/17.5 fl oz milk
5 egg yolks
salt and white pepper
6 egg whites
600 g/ 1 lb 5 oz whipping cream
200 g/7 oz Gruyère cheese (grated)

A cheese soufflé is an oven dish invented in eighteenth-century France. Under the influence of the heat, the air encapsulated in the bubbles of the stiffly beaten egg whites will expand. Soufflés made by insecure cooks often fail. They open the oven door to check if their creation is indeed rising gradually, but as a result of this action, cold air enters the oven, which can be detrimental to the entire process: the soufflé is doomed to collapse.

Preheat the oven to 200°C/392°F. Heat the milk in a saucepan and bring to the boil. Melt the butter in a thick-bottomed pan (for example, cast iron), whisk in the flour and keep stirring constantly for 1 minute. Then slowly add the milk, whisking constantly to prevent lumps. Cook for 3 minutes. Beat in the egg yolks and remove the pan from the heat. Add pepper and salt. Cover the pan with buttered baking paper, to avoid a skin forming on the top.

Beat the egg whites with a pinch of salt until they form firm, but not stiff, peaks. Add one third of the beaten egg whites to the yolk mixture and whisk them together into a smooth mixture. Then gently fold in the remaining egg whites. Place 4 tartlet moulds 8 cm/3.25 in in diameter onto 4 ovenproof plates and spoon the mixture into the moulds. Bake in the preheated oven for 4 minutes, until the soufflés have risen and the tops begin to turn golden. Pour the cream in a saucepan, heat gently, and add three quarters of the cheese. Keep stirring until the cheese has melted completely

into a smooth mixture. Do not boil! Carefully remove the moulds and soufflés from the plates. Pour the cream-cheese mixture on the plates and add the golden soufflés. Sprinkle the remaining grated cheese over the soufflés and put them briefly under the grill until the cheese has melted. Serve immediately.

Pan-fried skate wings with beurre noisette and capers

Jan Jansz van de Velde II (c. 1619-1662), **Still life with römer, flute glass, earthenware jug and pipes** *(1651).*

In the seventeenth century, olives were brought by ship from the Mediterranean area to the north. Shipwrecks were found near the Dutch shores with hundreds of olive jars aboard. Olives packed in olive oil kept for a long time. Olive cultivation is thousands of years old. Early on, the Romans developed methods of eliminating the bitter taste of olives. Today, various methods are used for this purpose: Spanish olives are fermented in an alkaline solution, and Greek olives are pickled in brine for half a year.

Even the very first Dutch-language cookbook, Een notabel boecxken van cokereyen *(A notable booklet of cooking), dating from 1514, contains a recipe for skate. The fish was first boiled and then stewed in vinegar and wine, and seasoned with nutmeg and saffron. And to make it even more exotic: 'some people sprinkle cinnamon on it when it is served at the table.'*

Preheat the oven to 185°C/365°F. Bring a pan of salted water to the boil, add the peeled potatoes and simmer until tender, about 15 to 16 minutes. Start the potatoes a few minutes before the fish, since the fish requires less cooking time. Heat the olive oil in a pan (with metal handles), large enough to accommodate all 4 skate wings. When the oil is well heated, fry the wings — one by one — for 1 to 2 minutes on each side. Then place the whole pan in the preheated oven for 6 to 7 minutes to finish cooking. Take the pan from the oven, using thick oven gloves. Put each skate wing on a plate. Add butter and wine vinegar to the drippings in the pan until the butter starts to turn brown (nut brown, hence the name 'beurre noisette'). Add the capers, squeeze in the lemon juice and finally add the chopped parsley. Pour the butter sauce over the skate wings and serve with the new, cooked potatoes.

ingredients for 4 servings

4 skate wings
750 g/1 lb 10.25 oz new potatoes (peeled)
200 g/7 oz unsalted butter
0.35 dl/1 generous fl oz red wine vinegar
2 lemons
50 g/1.75 oz capers
0.5 bunch parsley (chopped)
2.5 dl/8.75 fl oz olive oil

Upside down apple tart with vanilla crème fraîche

Cornelis Bisschop (1630-1674), **The apple peeler** *(1667).*

In the seventeenth century, the apples used in this recipe did not yet exist. In about 1825, the retired beer brewer, Richard Cox, planted seeds from a Ribston Pippin which he is thought to have pollinated with a Blenheim Orange apple. That was the advent of the Cox's Orange Pippin, one of the world's most famous apples, with annual sales exceeding € 150 million today. Cox's is an excellent dessert apple and suited for apple tart or pies.

ingredients for 4 servings

6 medium dessert apples preferably Cox's)

1 lemon

120 g/4.25 oz butter

200 g/7 oz sugar

300 g/10.5 oz ready-to-use puff pastry

Upside-down apple tart is called tarte tatin *in France. Originally it was called 'La tarte des demoiselles Tatin' (The Tatin spinsters' apple tart). They were two sisters, Caroline (1847-1811) and Stéphanie (1838-1917), who took over the hotel of their deceased parents in 1888, which was located in a castle in the town of Lamotte-Beuvron, south of Paris. The exact story is not known, but the most appealing version is that on an afternoon during hunting season, the absent-minded Stéphanie put the ingredients for an apple tart into the baking tin in the wrong order. She placed the baking tin in the oven and liked the result with the caramelized apples so much that she made this upside-down tart more often. The hotel still exists. So does the stove. As well as the baking tin.*

Preheat the oven to 220°C/428°F. Peel, halve and core the apples. Sprinkle them with lemon juice and place in the fridge. Grease the base of a frying pan evenly with butter and cover the bottom of the pan with sugar. Arrange the apples, round side down, on the bottom of the pan. Roll out the pastry dough on a lightly floured surface into a circle, about 3 mm/0.125 in thick. Place the sheet of pastry dough over the apples, allowing an overlap of about 2 cm/0.75 in. Trim off the excess with a pair of kitchen scissors, ensuring that the apples are evenly covered. Let the pan rest in the fridge for about 30 minutes. Then place the pan on fierce heat for about 15 to 20 minutes, until the butter and sugar are bubbling and have become a deep golden brown colour. Now place the pan

in the preheated oven and let the tarte tatin bake for 20 minutes, until the pastry has risen and is golden in colour. Remove the pan from the oven and leave to cool for 5 to 10 minutes. Turn over the tart so that the dough is on the bottom and the apples on top and serve with the vanilla crème fraîche.

Mix 3 drops of vanilla essence, scraped vanilla pods and crème fraîche into a smooth cream. If it's too sour, add a little powdered sugar to sweeten. Tip: put the scraped vanilla pods in a jar with sugar, seal with plastic wrap and leave it for a month. You'll then have delightfully fragrant sugar for coffee, sauces and desserts.

Ronald Kunis

'Cooking should be done with love.'

Restaurant De Kas

Kamerlingh Onneslaan 3

1097 DE Amsterdam

T 020 462 45 62

F 020 462 45 63

info@restaurantdekas.nl

www.restaurantdekas.nl

Ronald Kunis: 'When Gert Jan Hageman, who has more than earned his stripes in the kitchen, asked me to be the chef at the restaurant he was opening, I agreed right away. Every year we receive about 45,000 guests from all over the world.

'Our restaurant is located in a former Amsterdam Parks Department greenhouse, in the middle of a park. You're surrounded here by glass, which makes it seem as though you're outside. You see the sun go down and darkness fall. Lightning is spectacular. Rain and hail clatter against the glass. Here you can see the seasons go by, not only around you, but also on your plate. We use organic vegetables and free-range meat whenever possible. Close to the town of Purmerend we have our own plot of land, where we grow traditional vegetable sorts and varieties, and in the greenhouse itself we grow fruit, flowers and herbs. That includes nasturtium and violets; we use the leaves in salads. What's served here in the evening was harvested that same morning. A cook who works at De Kas is a bit of a farmer, a greengrocer, a fishmonger and a butcher.

'I make things the way they are. Ingredients should carry their own weight, that's much more important than the chef's "signature". We want the people who eat here to feel satisfied, and we make sure they leave the table feeling fresh and energetic.

'In our kitchen, everything revolves around the finesses, which means: an eye for detail. There are five or six of us working in the kitchen every day. It's hard work, because we start at ten in the

Ronald Kunis

morning and don't finish until around eleven in the evening. I'm not the kind of person who does all the fun things himself and leaves the nasty jobs to others. The more multifunctional the team, the more you can strive for refinement. The important thing is the pursuit of quality, each and every day, and to keep smiling, because we all greatly enjoy working here.

'Cooking takes time, and should be done with love. You can't cook potatoes faster by turning up the heat, and a tomato plant doesn't mature in a day.'

Frankenthaler grape focaccia, goat cheese and herb salad

ingredients for 4 servings

for the focaccia

600 g/1 lb 5 oz organic white wheat flour (and 3.5 oz for dusting)

3.5 dl/12.33 fl oz lukewarm water

0.8 dl/2.75 fl oz olive oil

15 g/0.5oz salt

25 g/0.75 oz fresh yeast (or 7 g/0.25 oz instant dry yeast)

grated zest of 1 lemon

1 tbsp fresh rosemary, coarsely chopped

1 tbsp thyme, chopped

1 tbsp brown sugar

1 bunch of blue grapes, preferably Frankenthaler (about 325 g/11.5 oz)

coarse sea salt

>>

Restaurant De Kas is situated in the former municipal greenhouse of the city of Amsterdam, in the Frankenthaler Park. Frankenthaler is an ancient grape variety that is again being cultivated by De Kas, and which is used in this focaccia recipe. Until the late nineteenth century, this sweet blue grape - originating from the East - was considered Holland's 'national' grape. In the eighteenth century, the grape was exported from Hamburg to England, which is why it is also known as Black Hamburg.

The focaccia Preheat the oven to 190°C/375°F. Weigh all the ingredients and have them ready to use. It is most satisfying to make the bread entirely by hand. It is quicker to use a food processor, but the result can not compare with the superior hand-made bread. Sift the flour into a large bowl and mix in the salt. Dissolve the yeast in lukewarm water. Ensure that the water is not warmer than body temperature, otherwise the yeast dies. Make a well in the centre of the sifted flour and pour into it the dissolved yeast and oil. Now mix the flour into the liquid, little by little, until it's all blended in. Then knead the dough, either in a bowl or on a floured surface, until it becomes a solid, pliable ball. The dough may be a bit moist. Lastly, mix in half of the chopped herbs and all of the lemon zest. Put the dough in a bowl, cover it, and let the dough rise in a warm place until doubled in size. Meanwhile, grease a baking tray or tart tin (about 28 cm/10 in in diameter) with some olive oil. When the dough has risen sufficiently, knock it back with your fists. Then

Karel Dujardin (1622-1678), **Italian landscape with woman milking a goat** *(1659).*

Evidently, the milk maid has been hard at work, because the herdsman is carrying a full tub of milk. Goat cheese was already consumed in ancient Rome. In fact, cheese-making is a good way to preserve milk. Strangely enough, during the Middle Ages and long after, cheese was considered to be unhealthy. Moreover, in the Middle Ages, goats got a bad name because they were associated with the devil, and later with poverty. Goats were only justly appreciated in the nineteenth century, when products derived from this animal graced the finest tables.

transfer it to the baking tray or tart tin, spreading it out to form a flat loaf. Divide the grapes over the bread and push them into the dough, sprinkle the bread generously with olive oil, the remaining herbs, brown sugar and a few grains of sea salt. Place a few whole sprigs of herbs on top of the bread for an extra dramatic effect. Let the bread rise once more to double its size and bake it in the pre-heated oven until golden brown and done, about 20-30 minutes. The bread is done if it sounds hollow when you knock on it or when an inserted toothpick comes out clean. The grapes are partially split and the sugar has melted across the bread. Remove the bread from the tin and let it cool on a wire rack. It's also delicious when reheated or toasted the next day.

for the salad

A few handfuls of seasonal herbs, if necessary supplemented with a variety of lettuce leaves
olive oil
garlic
freshly ground salt and pepper

1 mild goat cheese

The salad Prepare the herb salad using any seasonal herbs, if necessary mixed with a variety of lettuce leaves. Dress the salad with some good olive oil, finely crushed garlic, and freshly ground salt and pepper.

The presentation Cut off a wedge of bread, place it on a plate or wide bowl along with the salad, and add some soft goat cheese at room temperature. Sprinkle with a little more olive oil and pepper and sea salt.

Oyster and farmer's milk soup

with crostini topped with palm cabbage tartar and oysters

ingredients for 4 servings

For the oysters and crostini

12 oysters

bread, white or brown

olive oil

garlic

for the palm cabbage tartar

300 g/10.5 oz palm cabbage, rough veins and stems removed (if palm cabbage – the leaves of the palm tree – is not available, you can take kale or green cabbage instead)

0.5 clove garlic, finely chopped

1 tbsp capers, chopped

1 tbsp cornichons (small pickles), chopped

1 tbsp shallots, finely chopped

1 tbsp olives, chopped

1 tbsp parsley, chopped

4 tbsp olive oil

>>

It might seem strange, but soup with milk is basically the same as soup with cream. The milk is a splendid carrier for the oysters' briny taste. In the Middle Ages, milk was primarily used for making butter and cheese. People only started consuming milk as a beverage in the sixteenth and seventeenth centuries. Because it was considered to be bad for the teeth and gums, hence the advice: 'After consuming milk, make sure to rinse your mouth with wine.'

The palm cabbage tartar Bring a generous amount of water to the boil along with a good amount of salt (the taste of sea water) and cook the cabbage leaves in the water, a few at a time, until tender. Rinse quickly with cold water and squeeze out carefully. Chop the leaves into a 'tartar' and mix with garlic, capers, cornichons, shallots, olives, parsley, olive oil and lemon zest. Season with salt and freshly ground pepper.

The oysters Carefully open the fresh oysters (which have to smell delightfully fresh like the sea), using a good oyster knife or, if necessary, ask the fish supplier to do it for you.

The crostini Brush thick slices of (leavened) white or brown bread with some olive oil and bake it in a hot oven until golden brown and crisp. Sprinkle with salt, pepper and crushed garlic. Cover generously with palm cabbage tartar and serve immediately.

Nicolaes Maes (1634-1693), **Vegetable market** *(1655-1665).*

A sixteenth-century Dutch cookbook provides a recipe for stewing Savoy cabbage with marrow, raisins and ginger in hamelensop *(hamel = male sheep; sop = broth). Most likely, the word* hamelensop *was a general name for bouillon: 'Take the best heads of Savoy cabbage. When they are thoroughly washed, squeeze out all the water and place the marrow, raisins and ginger powder between the leaves, close them up again, to the best of your ability. Lay them in a pot with* hamelensop *and add ginger powder. Leave the cabbage to cook until done. Arrange on plates and serve at the table.'*

grated zest and juice of
0.5 lemon
freshly ground salt and pepper

for the soup

12 good-sized creuse oysters
(Japanese oysters)
7.5 dl/26.33 fl oz whole milk,
preferably farm-fresh
2 generous tbsp finely chopped
vegetable bouquet (e.g. leek,
onion, carrot, celeriac, garlic
and mushroom)
1 tbsp chervil or parsley
1 tbsp farm butter
salt and freshly ground pepper

The oyster soup Open the oysters. Be careful to catch all the oyster liquor and strain it to remove any bits of shell. Finely chop the oysters, keeping them separate from the liquor. Sweat the chopped vegetable bouquet in some olive oil. Add the oyster liquor and cook briefly at a low temperature. Add the milk and bring the soup to the boil. Taste the soup to see if it needs more salt. In any case, stir in a generous amount of freshly ground pepper. Add a pat of butter and beat the soup with a hand blender or whisk until foamy. Remove from the source of heat and mix in the chopped oysters, as well as the chervil and parsley. Serve the soup immediately in a bowl, with the crostini and oysters presented separately.

IJsselmeer pike-perch smoked in bay leaves

with crisp celeriac

ingredients for 4 servings

for the celeriac

- 1 beautiful, smooth celeriac, medium size
- a little fresh rosemary and thyme
- 1 clove garlic
- a dash olive oil
- 8 rashers of bacon or pancetta, thinly sliced

for the fish

- 1 pike-perch fillet (a thick steak); salmon is a good alternative
- chopped parsley
- lemon
- sea salt and freshly ground pepper

Celeriac, also called celery root, was already known in ancient Greece. In those days, the plant's leaves were made into wreaths and given to the dead to accompany them on their journey through the underworld. There are illustrations of Persephone, the wife of Hades, King of the Underworld, holding celeriac stalks in her hand. In the Netherlands, celeriac is mainly known as an indispensable ingredient of pea soup. But in this De Kas recipe, the vegetable has been resurrected in a surprising way.

The celeriac Wash the celeriac and peel thinly. Cut into 8 sections. Finely chop the rosemary, thyme and garlic. Transfer to a bowl and add a dash of olive oil. Dip the celeriac into the olive oil mixture until all sections are lightly but well covered. Wrap the sections in a slice of bacon or pancetta (according to preference), which you secure with a toothpick or metal skewer. Roast them slowly well above a barbecue until golden brown and tender. The art is to get the celeriac cooked and the bacon crisp at the same time. Celeriac really must be cooked thoroughly, not al dente, otherwise it does not taste good. It's a question of adjusting the grid up or down above the fire, as well as a little experience, of course. Celeriac can also be roasted in the oven: place the sections on a greased baking tray and roast them at 180°C/356°F until golden brown and thoroughly done. Season with some sea salt, freshly ground pepper and a drop of lemon. Whether prepared with or without bacon, celeriac tastes delicious served with all sorts of meat, poultry and fish, especially freshwater fish.

Harmen van Steenwijck (1612-1656), **Still life with earthenware jug, fish and fruit** *(1650).*

In the seventeenth century, it was more common to eat freshwater fish than today. Saltwater fish was known as 'sea fish' and freshwater fish simply as 'water fish'. In this painting, we see two bass and one pike-perch in a colander. Because of fasting, it was obligatory in Roman Catholic circles to eat fish on Wednesday, Friday and Saturday. An eighteenth-century cookbook dedicates an entire paragraph to the arrangement of dishes on the table for a three-course dinner, if 'Roman Catholics were invited on fish days'. From this, it can also be concluded that butter was eaten with bass and pike-perch.

The pike-perch Lightly smoke a thick, firm piece ofpike-perch above sawdust (ground wood shavings) and bay leaves. There is also a simpler method: grill or bake a nice, thick piece ofpike-perch and deglace with lemon juice combined with a tablespoon ofchopped parsley. Season to taste with lemon and olive oil, feshly ground pepper and sea salt. Serve with the celeriac.

Lemon and white bean soup

with poached sot-l'y-laisse of guinea fowl and chervil oil

Jan Jansz van de Velde (c. 1619-c. 1663), **Still life with tall beer glass** *(1647).*

In seventeenth-century cookbooks, we find recipes for lemon tart, lemon custard, lemon syrup, lemon confit, but there is also mention of limes as a tasty accompaniment to boiled pike. Certainly in the second half of the seventeenth century, exotic fruit was amply available. Pineapples were introduced in Europe thanks to the politician Pieter de la Court, whose gardener Willem de Vink cultivated them in his master's greenhouse. In a book written by De la Court's son in the early eighteenth century, he described how difficult it was 'to grow and multiply perfect pineapple fruits — as well as lemon, lime and orange trees and other plants from warmer regions — in our cold climes'.

Edwin Kats' amuse-gueule is a white bean soup with lemon and sot-l'y-laisse of guinea fowl. Sot-l'y-laisse (literally: the fool leaves it there) is considered to be the most delicious part of the bird, namely two small, oval-shaped morsels of meat in the pelvic cavity, which are difficult to find and remove.

The soup Soak the white beans for 24 hours in cold water. Then cook the beans with the lemon juice, poultry stock and cream until thoroughly done. Purée the soup in a food processor and strain through a sieve.

The oil Blanch the chervil and purée it for 10 minutes with the arachide oil. (Arachide oil is peanut oil.) Strain through a sieve.

The sot-l'y-laisses Poach the sot-l'y-laisses in the poultry stock and place them, equally divided, into 4 small coffee cups. Pour the hot white bean soup over them and finish with a few drops of chervil oil.

ingredients for 4 servings

for the soup

30 g/1 oz white beans

6 g/1 tbsp lemon juice

2 dl/7 fl oz poultry stock

1 dl/3.5 fl oz whipping cream

for the oil

25 g/0.75 oz fresh chervil

25 g/0.75 oz arachide oil

for the sot-l'y-laisses

8 sot-l'y-laisses of guinea fowl

1 dl/3.5 fl oz poultry stock

White grape and almond cream

with grilled langoustines and sage croûtons

ingredients for 4 servings

for the cream

juice of 500 g/1 lb 1.5 oz white grapes
10 g/0.33 oz crème fraîche
10 g/0.33 oz mascarpone
90 g/3.25 oz almond flakes
1 sheet gelatine
0.45 dl/1.5 fl oz whipping cream
salt

for the croûtons

12 bread croûtons
24 green asparagus tips
24 stalks celery
10 sage leaves
a few frisée leaves
olive oil

12 beautiful, large langoustines

A langoustine (or Norwegian lobster) is a small lobster with a maximum length of 25 cm/10 in in length. Langoustines are caught in the Mediterranean Sea, but especially in the North Sea and the east Atlantic Ocean as far south as the Moroccan coast. In Italy they are called scampi, a word that outside Italy often leads to confusion by referring to large prawns. Edwin Kats prefers langoustines from Loctudy, a fishing village in Brittany, where some 1,200 tons/2,688,000 lb) are caught every year. All langoustine catches brought ashore there receive the quality label 'La Demoiselle de Loctudy'.

The cream Put the grapes in a liquidizer, then bring to the boil and strain. Now add the dissolved gelatine, crème fraîche, mascarpone and salt and let it gel (stiffen) on ice water. Whip the cream and finely grind the almonds in a food processor. As soon as the grape mixture has set, add the whipped cream and let the mixture stiffen in the fridge for at least 3 hours.

The croûtons Roast the bread croûtons in olive oil together with 10 sage leaves until golden brown. Blanch the celery stalks and asparagus tips.

The langoustines Shell the langoustines and quickly fry them on both sides. Place them in a hot oven at 170°C/ 338°F for 2 minutes or until tender.

Balthasar van der Ast (1593/4-1657), **Still life with fruit and flowers** *(c. 1620/1).*

In the seventeenth century, grapes were mai nly culti - vated ƒr wi ne. On 6 Apri l 1652, Jan van Ri ebeeck, a nati ve ofCulemborg, took up resi dence i n South Afi ca where he supervi sed a settlement ofthe Dutch Uni ted East Indi a Company (VOC), whi ch used the Cape as a stopover port ƒr voyages to 'the East'. In 1654, he planted young grape cutti ngs, about 10 cm/4 i n long, ori gi nati ng fom the Rhi neland area. The ƒllowi ng year, he tri ed hi s luck at French grapes, whi ch were culti vated i nto the well-known steen grape and the sweet 'hanenpoot' (cock's ƒot), a grape that's also consumed as a fui t and whose Engli sh name i s 'honeypot!'. On 2 February 1659, Van Ri ebeeck wrote i n hi s logbook: 'Today, prai se be to God, wi ne was pressed ƒr the first ti me fom Cape grapes, and the fesh new wi ne was tasted fom the vat.' Thi s i s how the Dutch lai d the basi s ƒr South Afi can wi ne.

The presentation Arrange the langoustines and vegetables alternately on the plates, garnish the vegetables with a few tufts of frisée and spoon the cream into the centre.

Braised free-range pig's cheeks and feet

with green cabbage and shallot cream

ingredients for 4 servings

for the pig's cheeks and feet

4 pig's cheeks

8 pig's feet

1 litre/35.25 fl oz veal stock

for the pig's feet rolls

80 g/2.75 oz meat from the pig's feet

40 g/1.33 oz pig's feet skin

40 g/1.33 oz finely diced goose liver

20 g/0.66 oz reduced cooking liquid

for coating

1 egg white

arachide oil

butter

salt

pepper

for the cream

150 g/5.33 oz shallots

50 g/1.75 oz semi-whipped cream

>>

Braising means: to cook the food slowly in its own (or a small amount of) liquid or fat until tender. It's a cooking technique that was frequently used in the seventeenth century, not only to cook meat but also vegetables. Meat was first cooked in water until half done and afterwards braised in a closed pot suspended from a tripod above a slow (wood) fire.

The pig's cheeks and feet Sauté the cheeks and feet and cook them in veal stock for 3 hours over low heat until done. Cool the feet slightly and remove the meat from the bones. Weigh the required amount of meat, chop the skin finely. Keep the cheeks separately. Reduce 50 g/1.75 oz stock to 20 g/0.66 oz, mix with the feet, skin and the finely diced goose liver and wrap tightly into plastic film to get a nice smooth roll. Place the roll into the fridge for 6 hours to stiffen.

The cream Peel the shallots, chop them finely and cook them in the poultry stock until soft. Purée them into a smooth paste, heat them briefly and combine with the semi-whipped cream.

The cabbage Blanch the 4 green cabbage leaves, brush them with olive oil and dry them in an oven preheated to 80°C/176°F until crisp. Keep the oven door slightly ajar.

Sauté the green cabbage bâtonnets in 10 g/0.33 oz of butter.

Monogrammi st JVR, **Still life with pig's head, pig's feet and sausage**, *(1600-1650).*

The unknown pai nter si gned hi si ni ti als 'JVR' i n the bottom ri ght corner. Wri tten next to i t i s: 'It's all fom the pi g.' And, i ndeed, very fw parts ofthe pi g were di scarded; nearly everythi ng was processed i nto somethi ng edi ble. Accordi ng to the booklet De cierlijcke voorsnydinge aller tafelgerechten (The elegant way to carve all fods), publi shed i n 1664 by Hi eronymus Sweerts i n the Amsterdam Kalverstraat, i t was customary to first eat the neck and cheeks ofa wi ld boar's head. 'And i f these pi eces were i nsufi- ci ent, the ears were li fed up and a fw pi eces beneath them cut of but usually the ears are lef i n place fr ornamental reasons.' Somethi ng to please the eye. Then the wi ld boar meat was put on a plate and spri nkled wi th vi negar, wi th a bi t ofsalt on the si de.

The pig's cheeks and feet Cut the roll into 4 equal parts and coat them with a mixture consisting of beaten egg white, oil, salt and pepper. Cook them in 20 g/0.66 oz of arachide oil and 20 g/0.66 oz of butter until golden brown. Warm the cheeks in the stock.

The presentation Arrange all components attractively on a deep plate and garnish the dish with the dried green cabbage leaves.

for the cabbage

60 g/2 oz poultry stock

160 g/5.5 oz green cabbage bâtonnets

4 dried green cabbage leaves

Roast Dutch free-range chicken

with Jabugo ham, braised chicory and a creamy sauce with Oloroso Sherry

ingredients for 4 servings

for the free-range chicken

4 breast fillets of Dutch free-range chicken, with skin
2 beautiful slices Jabugo ham (if not available, use 'ordinary' Serrano ham)
80 g/2.66 oz thinly sliced Jabugo ham (if not available, use 'ordinary' Serrano ham)
4 sheets of pork net
10 heads chicory (Belgian endive)
100 g/3.5 oz butter
10 g/0.33 oz sugar
20 g/0.66 oz goose fat

for the sauce

80 g/generous 2.5 oz chicken wings
15 g/0.5 oz shallots, finely chopped
40 g/1/0.33 oz Oloroso Sherry
2 dl/7 fl oz poultry stock

>>

The seventeenth-century cookbook De verstandige Kock *(The sensible cook) offers numerous poultry dishes. In the Dutch Golden Age, a chicken was prepared as follows: 'Take a chicken. Roast it until half done. Take it off the spit. Take orange zest and cut it into quarters. Boil in water until half done. Fill a good-sized pan with acidic wine, add the orange zest and sugar to sweeten. Add the chicken and cook together until done. Serve together, and be sure to sprinkle with cinnamon.'*

The free-range chicken Soak the pork net for 24 hours and rinse well. Loosen and fold back the skin on one side of the fillet, sprinkle with pepper and salt and cover with the thinly sliced ham. Place the skin back and wrap the fillet in the pork net. Sauté the breast fillets carefully in 20 g/0.66 oz of goose fat. Transfer them to an oven preheated to 130°C/266°F for 12 minutes until tender. Slice the fillets just before serving.

The chicory (Belgian endive) Place the 2 slices of ham between 2 greaseproof papers in an oven preheated to 120°C/248°F for about 25 minutes until crisp. When the slices are removed from the oven, cut into 4 nice thin strips. Clean the heads of chicory and cook in 20 g/0.66 oz of butter and a little water until done. Remove them from the pan and halve them lengthwise. Sauté them in a non-stick pan with the butter and sugar until golden yellow and the sugar begins to caramelize.

Rembrandt van Ri jn (1606-1669), **Captain Frans Banningh Cocq gives his lieutenant the order for the company to march off** *(also known as* **The Night Watch***) (1642).*

She i s standi ng there i n fll li ght, even though she's defini tely not a ri fleman of the ri flemen's gui ld depi cted by Rembrandt. The fcal poi nt i s the chi cken sus-pended fom the gi rl's belt. In the seventeenth century, the Dutch word fr ri fle was 'clovere', deri ved fom 'claw'. That's why an eagle's claw could ofen be seen on the coats ofarms ofri fle-men's gui lds. Rembrandt opted fr a chi cken. As a result, the gi rl recei ved not only a symboli c but also a logi cal place i n the pai nt-i ng, namely that ofsutler: a woman selli ng fod to soldi ers.

1.5 dl/5 fl oz whipping cream

1 dl/3.5 fl oz Oloroso Sherry

1 pork net (available at the butcher)

The sauce To prepare the sauce, sauté the wings and shallots. Add 40 g/1/0.33 oz Oloroso Sherry and reduce (boil down). Add the poultry stock and cream and reduce to half the amount. Strain the sauce through a sieve and beat at once with a hand blender until foamy. Reduce 1 dl/3.5 fl oz of sherry until the liquid turns syrupy.

The presentation Arrange the sliced breast fillets on the plate so they overlap, place the chicory alongside, with the sauce and a few drops of reduced sherry in between. Add the crisp Jabugo ham for the finishing touch.

French toast

with fresh fruit tartar and raspberry curds

ingredients for 4 servings

24 rounds of brioche bread

for the fruit

60 g/2 oz mango

60 g/2 oz kiwi

60 g/2 oz papaya

60 g/2 oz pineapple

60 g/2 oz strawberries

60 g/2 oz melon

for the French toast batter

100 g/3.5 oz whipping cream

100 g/3.5 oz milk

3 eggs

60 g/2 oz powdered sugar

seeds of 1 vanilla pod

for the tuile (lit. curved roof tile)

60 g/2 oz butter

80 g/2.75 oz honey

115 g/4 oz sugar

120 g/4.25 oz flour

85 g/3 oz egg white

baking paper

>>

Brioche is a yeast bread made of flour, butter and eggs, somewhat resembling cake. When the French Queen Marie-Antoinette was told in the late eighteenth century that her subjects had no bread to eat, she supposedly asked: 'Qu'ils mangent de la brioche?' ('Let them eat cake!') Perhaps this comment was not as stupid and cruel as we may think today. Because in those days, bakers were obliged to sell the more expensive varieties of bread at the price of cheap bread if they had run out of the latter, so that flour was not used exclusively to produce luxury bread for the rich.

The raspberry curds Line a colander with cheese cloth, pour in the yoghurt, tie up the corners and let it hang for 12 hours to drain well. Purée the raspberries into a raspberry coulis (coulis is a liquid purée). Set aside 60 g/2 oz of coulis for the garnish. Blend the yoghurt with 100 g/3.5 oz of coulis and the sugar. Let the mixture set for 4 hours in the fridge.

The tuiles To prepare the tuiles (a sort of crisp biscuit), melt the honey and butter, then add the remaining ingredients. Pipe a stripe of batter onto a baking tray lined with greaseproof baking paper and bake the tuiles 6 minutes at 150°C/302°F.

The French toast Combine the cream, milk, eggs, powdered sugar and vanilla seeds into a batter. Dip the brioche rounds into the batter and fry them in 20 g/0.66 oz of arachide oil until golden.

Jan Havicksz. Steen (1626-1679), **Baker Arent Oostwaard and his wife Catharina Keizerswaard** *(c. 1658).*

Baker Arent Oostwaard and his wife show off their wares. The boy to the right is blowing a horn to announce that the bread is ready. The oblong-shaped bread is called a 'duivekater'(duive[l] = devil; kater = tom-cat). Such large, sweet breads are still being baked in some regions of the Netherlands as New Year's bread. The name's origin is not entirely clear. One of the interpretations is that the heathen Germanic people baked breads in the form of animals as an offering to the Gods, to put them in a benign mood. Christians named the bread 'duivelkater', not surprising since the cat was considered a diabolical animal.

The presentation Peel the fruit and cut everything into beautiful brunoises (small cubes). Arrange the fruit on the brioche rounds to create little tarts. Place a quenelle (little dumpling) of raspberry curds on each tart and top with a tuile. Surround each tart with a little raspberry coulis.

for the raspberry curds

500 g/17.5 oz yoghurt

raspberries for 160 g/5.66 oz raspberry coulis (purée)

125 g/4.5 oz sugar

Wil Demandt

'Cooks should actually read more.'

Restaurant Bordewijk

Noordermarkt 7

1015 MV Amsterdam

T 020 624 38 99

F 020 420 66 03

Wil Demandt: 'Every chef has his own reasons for choosing this profession. My mother was a very bad cook. Terrible. When I was twelve, I said to her: "You know what? Let me do the cooking from now on. That's a better idea." Later, I studied history at school, but I enjoyed cooking so much that I decided to become a cook. We started Bordewijk in 1985. Some of our customers have been coming here right from the beginning. Some of them even came here with their parents, and now that they're grown up they come in themselves.

'A good cook has stamina and brains. You can learn to cook by trying out lots of things. You have to do a lot of tasting. And especially a lot of reading. I get my information from a variety of sources. I think cooks should actually read a lot more books. Cooks who can read know their classics, and know that there isn't much new under the sun. The Frenchman Bocuse once said that you're a very important cook if you come up with one truly new thing in your life. Coming up with a new dish is not merely making a zabaglione and adding tarragon to it: inventing zabaglione, *that* is an innovation. It would be a mistake to think that the great dishes arose in a wave of inspiration. They usually arose from the fact that someone had little choice.

'But I'm more interested in the history of dishes than in innovations. Dutch local recipes are what's near and dear to me. For this book, I went looking for things that fit with the paintings

Wil Demandt

and with the period of time when they were painted.

'I try to buy as many of my products as possible here in the neighbourhood. Then they're good and fresh. This work is never the same from one day to the next, even if only because the products you use are never the same. Our guests keep me guessing as well. Not too long ago, one of them actually left me flabbergasted. He had just eaten a lovely dessert with a hundred grams of sugar and a hundred grams of butter in it, and then he asked for bonbons along with the coffee.'

Warm oysters with sour cream and nutmeg

Hendrik Cornelisz. Vroom (c. 1566-1640), **Return to Amsterdam of the second expedition to the East Indies, 19 July 1599** *(1599).*

The Mauritius returned from Bantam with a ship loaded with pepper. Meanwhile, four other Dutch ships sailed from Bantam to the Moluccas to collect the new harvest of nutmeg, mace and cloves. The Banda Islands were the main suppliers of these spices. Actually, mace is the outer covering surrounding the nutmeg seed, meaning that these two spices grow on the same tree. The fragile seeds were easily damaged when they knocked against each other and rotted away before they had a chance to ripen. Ripe seeds were harvested with great care, either by hand or with a stick to which a net and hook were attached, also called 'gaai-gaai'. For more than one and a half centuries, the Dutch United East India Company ruled the world trade in these spices. To protect their position, they destroyed nutmeg trees found in other regions. The spices were transported in convoys of 15 ships. The Dutch United East India Company made a profit of about 25,000 guilders per ship.

The custom of grating nutmeg over oysters is rather old. The people of Zeeland already did so in the Dutch Golden Age, most likely to mask the taste of somewhat older specimens. In the seventeenth century, French cooks added nutmeg to nearly everything. And, as if this weren't enough, diners liked to carry their own little grater and nutmeg kernel for that extra touch. To ensure that the kernels wouldn't germinate during transport on the ships of the Dutch United East India Company (VOC), they were rubbed with lemon juice, which made their colour fade. Nutmeg is still being bleached that way, although today this is not strictly necessary.

ingredients for 4 servings

- 16 oysters (creuse or Zeeland flat oysters)
- freshly ground pepper
- nutmeg (and a grater)
- 200 g/7 oz crème fraîche or sour cream
- sea salt
- leavened bread

Preheat the oven to 250°C/482°F. Open the oysters. Leave them in the half shell, and cover each oyster with a teaspoon of sour cream. Top with a grating of nutmeg and some freshly ground pepper. Place the oysters on little mounds of sea salt in an ovenproof dish, and slide it in the oven for about 3 minutes. Serve when the oysters and the liquid feel warm but are still raw. Serve with a slice of leavened bread.

Jellied skate and crisp bacon

with a warm shallot vinaigrette

ingredients for 4 servings

for the jelly

1 kg/2 lb 3.33 oz skate wings
salt pepper
50 g/1.75 oz capers
50 g/1.75 oz chopped parsley
10 g/0.33 oz chopped lemon confit
1 dl/3.5 fl oz white wine vinegar
5 dl/17.5 fl oz water

for the bacon

4 rashers thinly sliced bacon (not smoked)

for the vinaigrette

50 g/1.75 oz chopped shallots
2 tbsp red wine vinegar with bay leaf
2 dl/7 fl oz olive oil salt pepper

A vinaigrette is the simplest sauce there is. It is made of two main ingredients that can not be mixed, namely oil and vinegar. The vinegar remains visible in the form of small droplets, scattered throughout the oil. In England, vinaigrette is also called 'French dressing'. The literary gourmet Jean-Anthelme Brillat-Savarin (1755 - 1826) tells about a French salad maker who came to London completely destitute and made a fortune with his salads. He was chauffeured around the city in his own carriage, accompanied by a servant who carried a mahogany box containing 'various kinds of vinegar, all sorts of oil' and other ingredients.

The jelly Poach the skate with all the ingredients on a gentle fire for about 20 minutes until done. Remove the skate from the cooking liquid. Take the meat off the bones in large pieces and put it back into the bouillon. Season to taste; remember that it will be eaten cold, so use a little more salt than usually! Add the parsley when the bouillon begins to gel (thicken) and pour it into 4 small moulds. Let them cool in the fridge for about 2 hours.

The bacon Fry the bacon slowly in a frying pan until crisp (gentle fire!).

The vinaigrette Cook the shallots with the oil, vinegar, salt, pepper and bay leaf gently for 10 minutes. Keep warm.

The presentation Turn a mould of jellied skate onto each plate and let it reach room temperature (about 20 minutes).

Ludolf Bakhuysen (1631-1708), **Stormy sea with Dutch ship under full sail** *(1694).*

Fishermen risked their lives to catch what Dutch people enjoyed eating as fresh as possible: fish. This was no easy feat in the seventeenth century. Large country houses usually had a spacious ice cellar where the ice 'harvested' in winter from nearby lakes or ponds was used all summer long to cool food. The ice was also used to cool white wine; even snow was conserved for this purpose. Cooling wine in snow was considered very trendy. Fish and meat were frequently preserved by means of jellying. Skate as prepared in Restaurant Bordewijk's recipe could be kept in a cool cellar for several days.

Top it with the crisp bacon and surround it with the vinaigrette. Serve with a small green salad, if desired.

Skate prepared this way could be kept in a cool cellar for a few days. And it was very tasty. In the pre-refrigerator era, jellying was a method of preserving meat and fish.

Ravioli with pumpkin and sage butter

Pieter de Hooch (1629-after 1683), **Three women and a man in a courtyard behind a house** *(1663-1665).*

The late summer colours of the sun on the bricks and roof tiles inspired Restaurant Bordewijk to create this recipe bursting with Indian Summer flavours. In the painting, we see a maid with a pot getting rain water from a barrel, while a young woman is squeezing out a lemon above her sweet white wine, a young man is smoking a pipe, and a third woman is standing with a glass of beer in her hand. Curious what they'll be eating soon?

ingredients for 4 servings

for the filling

1 organically grown, orange pumpkin of 400 g/14 oz
3 cloves garlic, peeled and chopped
2 onions, chopped
150 g/5.33 oz butter
2 bay leaves
5 sage leaves, chopped
salt
pepper

for the pasta dough

500 g/1 lb 1.5 oz hard wheat flour ('00')
25 g/0.75 oz semolina made from durum wheat
4 eggs
about 0.5 cup water

for the butter

150 g/5.33 oz butter
10 g/0,33 oz sage leaves, chopped

>>

It is known that about 25 pumpkin species have been cultivated for more than 9,000 years. The pumpkin is an annual plant and belongs to the cucumber and courgette family. The giant American pumpkins are traditionally hollowed out for Halloween. The meat of the pumpkin is used in a variety of dishes: from hearty soups to sweet desserts.

The filling Cut the pumpkin in half and scoop out the seeds. Chop the meat into pieces. Sauté the onions and garlic in the butter, then add the pumpkin, sage, pepper, salt and bay leaves. Cover the pan and cook on a gentle fire into a pulp (the pulp must not be too wet; if so, remove the lid to let the moisture steam off briefly). Set aside to cool and remove the bay leaves.

The dough Knead the flour, eggs and water into a pasta dough. Let it rest in plastic wrap for 1 hour. Dust a surface with semolina and roll out the dough into sheets about 2 mm/0.75 in thick, 12 cm/4.75 in wide, and 30 cm/12 in long (in other words, the second last setting on the pasta machine). Let the dough dry a little. Then brush the sheets of dough, one at a time, with the beaten egg white. Spoon small dollops of the pumpkin filling onto the sheet at regular intervals. Cover with a second sheet of pasta dough (on top of the pumpkin mounds). Pat down the dough between the mounds of filling. Carefully cut out each ravioli with a fluted pastry wheel. Press the edges down firmly and put them on a platter dusted with

semolina. The ravioli can easily be frozen.

The cooking Bring the salted water to the boil. Add the ravioli and cook for 3 to 4 minutes, or until the dough is al dente.

The presentation Meanwhile warm a serving dish, put the pats of butter in it and the chopped sage. Spoon the cooked ravioli with the attached moisture into the dish and mix well. Season with freshly ground pepper and serve immediately while hot!

salt

freshly ground black pepper

5 litres water

100 g/3.5 oz salt

1 egg white, beaten

Seven-hour goose

Jan Baptist Weenix (1621-c. 1660), **A monkey and a dog with dead game and fruit** *(1714).*

In De verstandighe kock (The sensible cook) the recipe for roast goose is preceded by a suggestion for 'taking away the greasy taste'. 'Take a well-cleaned goose. Put a turmeric root into the cavity.' Then the goose has to be cooked for 2 hours. Now remove the turmeric. Put the goose on a spit and roast until done. 'You will find there is no taste of greasiness at all.

It's hard to imagine, but about one and a half centuries ago the majority of the Dutch population were still cooking on an open fire, above which a pot was suspended. Stoves with several burners and an oven were only available in the nineteenth century and that meant an end to kettle meals, the one-pot casseroles. And finally, it became possible to put a goose in the oven and let it cook slowly there for 7 hours.

The goose Salt the inside and outside of the goose a day in advance. Put all herbs in the stomach cavity together with the onion. Next day, put the goose in the oven on a rack with the dripping pan underneath. Set the oven to 90°C/194°F. Keep basting the goose with the pan drippings during the entire 7 to 8 hours of cooking time and you'll slowly get confit of goose. For the last hour, the halved, cored quinces filled with chestnut-purée, butter and sugar join the goose fat in the dripping pan. When the goose is cooked, remove it from the oven; check with a toothpick for doneness. Let the goose rest for about 1 hour. Remove the quinces from the goose fat and keep them warm. Set the oven to a high temperature, baste the goose again with the drippings and let the skin of the goose get nice and crisp (about 5 minutes).

Ingredients for 4 servings

for the goose

1 beautiful, young, fat goose, about 2.5 kg/4 lb 7 oz (preferably from Bresse)

1 onion

salt

pepper

bay leaf

thyme

rosemary

for the quince

4 quinces

200 g/7 oz chestnut purée from a tin (or home-made)

50 g/1.75 oz butter

100 g/3.5 oz sugar

French toast made of Frisian cinnamon bread

with coconut ice-cream

ingredients for 4 servings

for the French toast

4 slices cinnamon bread

1 egg

2 dl/7 fl oz milk

75 g/2.5 oz butter

powdered sugar

for the ice-cream

1 tin coconut milk, about 4 dl/14 fl oz

the juice and chopped meat of 1 fresh coconut (can be bought at a Chinese shop)

6 egg yolks

100 g/3.5 oz sugar

How to kill a coconut? The coconut shell has three 'eyes'. Bore a whole through the softest of the three eyes and drain the coconut water into a bowl. Place the coconut into an oven preheated to 180°C/356°F. The nut will crack open after about half an hour. A blow with a hammer also might help, preferably applied to the side with the three 'eyes'. Scrape out the meat with a spoon.

The ice-cream Mix the coconut milk with the fresh coconut water. Heat to 90°C/194°F. Beat the egg yolks with the sugar until foamy. Add the coconut mixture and stir until it resembles a thick cream. Put this cream in an ice-cream maker, adding a few small pieces of fresh coconut meat.

The French toast Beat the egg with the milk and dip the slices of cinnamon bread into the mixture. Fry in butter at a low temperature, turning the bread over several times. Sprinkle with powdered sugar and serve with the coconut ice-cream.

Andries Beeckman (17th century), **The view of the castle of Batavia, seen from Kali Besar West** *(c. 1656-1658).*

Men are picking the coconuts from the palm trees with long sticks. The coconuts we buy at our local shop are actually the pit of a much larger fruit. But the nut with its meat and milk are not the only useful parts of the coconut palm. In the seventeenth century, (and much longer before that, of course) the shells were used for making spoons and cups, the leaves for roof covering and the wood for building ships. And the branches of the tree produced a liquid, the so-called palm wine, which the islanders processed into arrack.

Tony Philippi

'Here, people eat things they don't eat at home.'

Restaurant

Voorbij het Einde

Sumatrakade 613

1019 PS Amsterdam

T 020 419 11 43

F 033 479 31 92

aperlot@wxs.nl

www.voorbijheteinde.nl

Tony Philippi: 'We opened in 2001. I own the business. I really wanted to do something new, so I decided to start a restaurant on Java Island. Because it was all new construction here, I was able to say exactly how I wanted it. For a cook, it's an absolute luxury to be able to design your own kitchen.

'Before this, I had all kinds of jobs. As cook on a Navy vessel, for example. I also worked as a valet to Princess Juliana and Prince Bernhard. A unique experience. The contact with them was very close. Prince Bernhard would sometimes call me at home. He'd be working on a crossword puzzle and he needed help. "Listen, Philippi: English musical genre, three letters?" And I'd say: "Ska, your royal highness." And he'd say: "Philippi, I am indebted." It taught me a lot about working on the other side of the counter. When you start for yourself, that kind of experience with serving comes in quite handy. There at Soestdijk Palace I also gained experience as a wine steward, because every bottle that's opened has to be tasted first. But then the wine-tasting is as good as it gets.

'I learned cooking from Rudolf Bos, during my four years at Mangerie de Kersentuin. Of course, you have to have a natural ability for it. You don't become a cook just like that. You have to learn how to do all those things at once. You're busy with both your hands and your head all the time. There are so many things that have to be done at the same time. You have to have that in you. But cleaning and cooking a lobster, for example, is something you can't

Tony Philippi

teach yourself. If you've seen it once or twice, then you know how to do it, but top cuisine is not something you can teach yourself.

'When you try my recipes for this book, you'll probably find that it doesn't all go by itself the first time 'round. But if you keep trying, it will finally turn out right. I do a lot of experimenting myself. You have to develop a feeling for that. A soufflé doesn't just happen by itself. Dutch people should really pay a bit more attention to things like that. Going out for Chinese or pizza is not a culinary achievement. Which is the whole idea behind this restaurant — here, people eat things they don't eat at home. The same goes for me: at home I tend to make mashed potatoes with endives and a cut of bacon. Things like that. I love real Dutch home-cooking.'

Scallops wrapped in marinated wild salmon

with blood orange and lobster vinaigrette

ingredients for 4 servings

for the salmon

1 kg/2 lb 3.5 oz centre cut of wild salmon with skin
0.5 bunch dill
0.5 bunch coriander
0.5 bunch tarragon
40 g/1.33 oz sea salt
25 g/scant 1 oz brown sugar
15 g/0.5 oz crushed pepper corns
10 g/0.5 oz crushed coriander seeds
juice and grated zest of 1 orange
juice and grated zest of 1 lime

for the scallops

4 large, cleaned scallops
olive oil
2 cloves garlic
1 shallot
2 sprigs tarragon
2 sprigs coriander
2 sprigs dill
sea salt
pepper >>

Nowadays we marinate food to add flavour, but originally it was a way of preserving food for longer periods of time. By adding an acidic substance such as vinegar to fish, for example, the growth and multiplication of harmful microorganisms can be prevented. Conversely, another method of food preservation is to add a substance that will generate the growth of acid-forming bacteria. The word 'ketchup' is derived from the Chinese word 'ke-tsiap' and means 'pickled fish sauce' (and has the same origin as the Indonesian soy sauce called ketjap). In seventeenth-century England, it was a term referring to sauce of fermented mushrooms or walnuts. Today, we take it to mean tomato pulp pickled in vinegar.

The salmon Coarsely chop the herbs and combine them with the other ingredients, with the exception of the lime juice, orange juice and salmon. Place the salmon, skin side down, on a platter and cover with the herb mixture. Squeeze the lime and orange over the salmon. Cover it tightly with aluminium foil and let it marinate in the fridge for 24 hours.

Clean the salmon and put it in olive oil for about 1 hour. Pat it dry thoroughly with kitchen paper, then cut the fish into slices as thin and long as possible.

The scallops Cut each scallop into 5 thin slices and marinate them in olive oil combined with the remaining ingredients for about 1.5 hours prior to serving.

Hendrick Martensz. Sorgh (c. 1611-1670), **The female fish vendor** *(1650-1670).*

The seventeenth-century classic The Compleat Angler *by Izaak Walton contains a chapter about salmon: 'Observations of the Salmon; with Directions how to fish for him', in which the salmon is presented as the 'king of freshwater fish'. At the end of the chapter, Walton praises the salmon to the skies. If you catch a salmon, you'll see that its body is adorned with black spots that emphasize its natural beauty, 'as I think was never given to any woman by the artificial paint and patches in which they so much pride themselves in this age.'*

for the salad

4 blood oranges
1 head frisée lettuce (only the light heart)
dill sprigs
coriander leaves
tarragon
purple basil leaves
olive oil
fine sea salt
pepper

for the vinaigrette

1 dl/3.5 fl oz olive oil
1 dl/3.5 fl oz cold lobster stock
4 blood oranges
honey
0.2 dl/0.75 fl oz raspberry vinegar
2 sprigs coriander
2 sprigs dill
2 sprigs tarragon
2 cloves garlic
1 shallot

The salad Peel and segment the blood oranges. Pick the leaves off the frisée (avoiding the hard white core and the dark green leaves), wash and dry them well. Mix the frisée with the herbs and the blood oranges. Dress with the lobster vinaigrette.

The vinaigrette Squeeze out the 4 blood oranges and boil the juice with a little honey, sprigs of herbs, raspberry vinegar, garlic and shallot until reduced to half the amount. Strain through a fine-meshed sieve and let it cool. Take a hand blender and mix in the olive oil and the cold lobster stock and season to taste with sea salt and pepper.

Lobster tail poached in watercress bouillon

with lobster soufflé and watercress sabayon

Pieter de Ring (1615-1660), **Still life with a golden goblet** *(1640-1660).*

According to some sources, lobsters were not caught in our waters during the seventeenth century, but rather in more northern parts of the North Sea. The lobsters we now find in the waters around Zeeland are said to be descendants of specimens that had escaped in those days. Most chefs cook a lobster while it's still alive to prevent loss of flavour, while others prefer putting it in a freezer for 1 hour to dull its senses.

ingredients for 4 servings

for the bouillon

3 dl/10.5 fl oz white wine
1 large bunch watercress
3 shallots
4 cloves garlic
1 small leek
5 dl/17.5 fl oz water
sea salt and pepper

for the lobster tail

2 whole lobsters of 450 g/1 lb each
1 winter carrot
1 leek
2 onions
celery
1 bulb garlic
1 tbsp tomato paste
3 dl/10.5 fl oz white wine
1 litre/35.25 fl oz water

for the soufflé

0.5 dl/1.75 fl oz cold lobster stock
pieces of lobster claw meat >>

Sabayon is a French version of the Italian 'zabaglione'. One of the legends about its origin goes as follows: Pascual Baylón (1540 - 1592) was a Spanish shepherd who in 1582 entered a Franciscan monastery. In a church in Turin, he recommended a recipe to women who confessed to him about their less than 'ardent' husbands, providing them with a memory aid, namely 1+2+2+1: beat 1 egg yolk with 2 tsp sugar until foamy and add 2 egg shells of marsala (a dark dessert wine) and 1 egg shell of water. Stir above a low fire. In the Piedmontese dialect spoken in Turin, the Spanish friar's name became 'sanbajon' and that word was corrupted into 'zabaglione'. San Baylón is the patron saint of bakers and cooks. His name day is on 17 May.

The bouillon Combine white wine, watercress, shallots, garlic, leek, water, sea salt and pepper in a pan and let the bouillon simmer gently for 1.5 hours. Strain through a fine-meshed sieve and then reduce the bouillon to a quarter of its volume.

The lobster tails Chop and wash all vegetables and put them together with the tomato paste in a pan with hot olive oil. Deglace with white wine and water and bring to the boil. Then cook the lobster for 4 minutes until done. Rinse the lobster well until cold and pull out the tail and claws. Place the shells and residue back into the bouillon and cook it for about 2 hours at a low temperature. Strain through a fine-meshed sieve and reduce into a strong lobster

stock. Cut the lobster tails lengthwise. Remove the meat from the claws. It will be used for the salad and the soufflé. Before serving, poach the lobster tails in a fireproof dish with the watercress bouillon for 4 minutes at 80°C/176°F.

The soufflé Preheat the oven to 200°C/392°F. Melt the butter and generously grease 4 ramekins (individual ovenproof dishes) with a brush, from bottom to top. Beat the egg whites with a little sea salt until very stiff and fold the cold lobster stock into the stiff egg whites. Add the pieces of lobster claw meat, and divide the mixture over the 4 buttered ramekins. Bake immediately at 200°C/392°F for 4 minutes.

The sabayon Reduce the watercress bouillon to half its volume and set aside to cool. Then add the egg yolk and whisk on a very low fire until it becomes a nice, foamy mass. Do not allow the egg yolks to curdle. Now add the clarified butter and the watercress leaves. Season to taste with fine sea salt and pepper.

3 egg whites
fine sea salt
20 g/0.66 oz butter
ramekins

for the sabayon

1 dl/3.5 fl oz watercress bouillon
10 g/0.33 oz small watercress leaves
3 egg yolks
10 g/0.33 oz clarified butter
fine sea salt
pepper

for the garnish

watercress leaves
sundried pomodori
olive oil
a few pieces of reserved lobster claw meat

Roast wild boar with parsnip mousseline

and sauerkraut spring roll with bay leaf gravy

ingredients for 4 servings

for the wild boar fillet

0.5 bunch sage
0.5 bunch rosemary
0.5 bunch lemon thyme
3 cloves garlic
10 g/0.33 oz crushed pepper corns
20 g/0.66 oz sea salt
10 g/0.33 oz crushed coriander seeds
grated lemon zest
grated orange zest
1 kg/2 lb 3.33 oz wild boar fillet
butter
oil
veal juice

for the mousseline

400 g/14 oz Opperdoes potatoes
5 large parsnips
200 g/7 oz butter
2.5 dl/8.75 fl oz skim milk

>>

After a Scottish physicist discovered in about 1750 that citrus fruits prevented scurvy, ships made a habit of loading up on huge quantities of citrus fruits during their voyages - even though it was not yet known at the time that it was the vitamin C in these fruits that combated the disease. In those days, they also discovered that scurvy did not occur on ships where sauerkraut was eaten regularly (also due to its high vitamin C content). From that time on, it was obligatory to eat sauerkraut on board ships at least once a week. Cabbage was originally pickled in China and brought to Europe by the Tartars (Mongols).

The wild boar Finely chop the herbs and garlic and mix them with the remaining ingredients. Spread this mixture on a piece of aluminium foil and roll the boar fillet in it. Place the meat on a platter in the fridge and turn it over from time to time. After 24 hours, clean the boar fillet and pat it dry with kitchen paper. Sear the wild boar fillet in plenty of butter and oil until well browned on all sides and continue to cook until its core temperature reaches 45°C/113°F. Reduce some veal juice until it starts to gel (thicken) and glaze the wild boar fillet with it.

The mousseline Peel the parsnips, then quarter 1 parsnip lengthwise. Sauté the quartered parsnip in some goose fat until golden brown, then add the remaining goose fat. Continue to cook slowly at 70°C/158°F until al dente. Peel the potatoes and cut the rest of

Joos de Momper (1564-1635), **River landscape with boar hunt** *(c. 1590-1635).*

Wild boar hunting is notoriously dangerous. In Ovid's Metamorphoses, *we find an account of a hunt for a huge boar sent by Diana, Goddess of the Hunt, after King Oeneus had neglected to honour her with an offering, even though the first grain of the new harvest had been dedicated to Ceres, the first wine to Bacchus and the olive oil to Minerva. The wild boar Diana had sent out of vengeance was an immensely dangerous animal, as massive as a bull. A whole army of heroes and hounds were summoned but failed to kill the boar and perished in the process. The girl Atalanta was the first one able to injure the animal with an arrow. Ultimately, it was Meleager who succeeded in killing the boar with a spear and a hunting knife.*

the parsnips into chunks. Cook them in a generous amount of sea-salted water until tender. Rub through a fine-meshed sieve. Bring the milk to the boil and add to the purée. Stir in the butter and some coarse pepper before serving.

The spring rolls Rinse the sauerkraut with cold water. Drain well. Put the remaining ingredients up to and including the wild flower honey in a pan together with the sauerkraut. Cook the sauerkraut at a low temperature until it reaches the doneness desired. Let the sauerkraut cool and drain thoroughly. Mix the sauerkraut with some crème fraîche and divide it over the spring roll sheets. Roll up the spring roll sheets evenly, flour the open sides and then dip them first into the egg white and then into the grated hazelnuts. Let the spring rolls rest in the freezer for about 2 hours. Deep fry the spring rolls in sunflower oil at 170°C/338°F.

The gravy Cook the old port together with the shallot, juniper berries and garlic until reduced to half. Now add the veal stock, maple syrup and bay leaves and reduce again to half the amount. Strain the gravy (preferably through a cloth but a fine-meshed sieve will also do) and season to taste.

sea salt
coarse pepper
2 dl/7 fl oz goose fat

for the spring roll

400 g/14 oz sauerkraut
small piece smoked bacon
3 juniper berries
1 clove
1 shallot
1 clove garlic
2 sprigs bay leaf
1 dl/3.5 fl oz Noilly Prat (Vermouth)
1 tsp wild flower honey
6 spring roll sheets, 15 cm x 15 cm/6 in x 6 in
50 g/1.75 oz grated hazelnuts
1 egg white
a little flour
sunflower oil
1 tbsp crème fraîche

for the gravy

2 dl/7 fl oz old red port
2 dl/7 fl oz strong veal stock
1 tsp maple syrup
1 shallot
2 cloves garlic
2 juniper berries
8 bay leaves
pepper and sea salt

White chocolate-lavender parfait

with chocolate volcano and lavender oublies

Dirck van Valkenburg (1675-1721), ***Plantation in Suriname*** *(1707).*

In 1706, the Amsterdam merchant Jonas Witsen commissioned Dirck van Valkenburg to travel to Suriname to paint his plantations there. This painting is the earliest dated work painted in Suriname. The Dutch had already established themselves in Suriname some time ago. Cornelis van Aerssen van Sommelsdijck (1637-1688) arrived in late 1683 as governor in Paramaribo (which in those days consisted of just a few dozen houses). He stimulated the construction of cacao plantations. The beans were processed in the Netherlands into chocolate, which was initially drunk for medicinal purposes. The rich cacao butter was used as hand cream and lip balm, and as raw material for the production of soap.

ingredients for 4 servings

for the mousse

150 g/5.33 oz valrhona chocolate
2.5 dl/8.75 fl oz whipping cream
1 egg yolk
4 egg whites
15 g/0.5 oz butter
75 g/2.5 oz sugar
0.25 dl/scant 1 fl oz water
0.1 dl/0.33 fl oz Pedro Ximinez

for the chocolate biscuits

115 g/4 oz butter
100 g/3.5 oz brown caster sugar
100 g/3.5 oz white caster sugar
150 g/5.33 oz chocolate chips
100 g/3.5 oz almonds
1 egg
155 g/5.5 oz flour

>>

When in 1519 the Spanish conqueror Hernan Cortés landed in today's Mexico, the Aztecs believed that one of their gods had arrived. Cortés made clever use of their confusion and asked the Indians to relinquish their most precious possessions. They promptly took him to a plantation and presented him with mountains of cacao beans. Their greatest treasure. Cortés himself had been thinking more in terms of mountains of gold, but once he tasted the nectar they prepared from the beans, he felt quite reconciled. Because the 'tchocoatl' came in a golden cup and was served by a nude virgin.

The mousse Melt the chocolate in a bain-marie together with the butter. Whip the cream lightly (as you do for Irish coffee) and put it in the fridge. Combine the sugar and water in a small pan and cook until syrupy, but do not let it start to caramelize. Beat the egg whites and slowly add the sugar syrup, preferably using a food processor with a whisk. Beat energetically until stiff peaks have formed. Blend together one quarter of the whipped cream, chocolate and beaten egg whites with a scraper and then fold in the rest of the recipe. Fill a piping bag with the mixture and squirt into the baskets.

The biscuits Combine the butter with the soft white and brown sugar, add the egg and the flour and mix well. Chop the almonds and chocolate into small pieces and stir into the batter. Divide the batter into small, round balls and bake them on a tray lined with baking paper for 8 minutes at 165°C/329°F. Let the biscuits cool.

The baskets Melt the chocolate and butter. Finely crush the biscuits and combine with the chopped pecans, sugar, cacao and brandy. Add the melted chocolate and butter and combine well. Fill the aluminium tins by gently covering the bottom and the sides with the mixture. Try to apply an attractive, thin and even layer. Set them aside in the fridge. Use a piping bag to fill the baskets with chocolate mousse, try to squirt a volcano on top using a smooth nozzle and let it stiffen in the fridge for about 1 hour. Then cut the aluminium tin open and carefully remove it from the chocolate volcano.

The parfait Melt the chocolate in a bain-marie, whip the cream lightly (as you do for Irish coffee). Place the sugar and water together in a small pan and cook until syrupy, but do not let it start to caramelize. Beat the egg yolks and the whole egg and slowly add the sugar syrup, preferably using a food processor with a whisk. Beat energetically until a nice, firm froth has formed. Blend together one quarter of the whipped cream, chocolate and beaten egg whites with a scraper and then fold in the rest of the recipe. Divide the parfait over the 4 rings and place in the freezer for about 8 hours.

The oublies Melt the butter and mix with the remaining ingredients of this recipe. Allow the mixture to stiffen in the fridge for half an hour. Spread the batter into the stencil placed on a (silicon) baking mat. Bake the oublies about 12 minutes at a temperature of 125°C/257°F and, while still warm, roll them around a ring with a diameter of 5 cm/2 in. Let them cool. Before serving, fill the oublies with the parfait.

for the chocolate baskets

200 g/7 oz chopped pecans
200 g/7 oz chocolate biscuits (see recipe above)
2 tsp cacao
1.5 tbsp brown sugar
2 tbsp brandy
60 g/2 oz butter
80 g/2.75 oz dark chocolate
disposable aluminium tins, about 6 cm x 6 cm/2.33 in x 2.33 in

for the parfait

4 egg yolks
1 whole egg
75 g/2.5 oz sugar
2.5 dl/8.75 fl oz water
2 dl/7 fl oz whipping cream
100 g/3.5 oz white chocolate
200 g/7 oz finely chopped lavender
4 round, open rings, 9 cm/3.5 in high, with a diameter of about 4 cm/1.5 in

for the oublies

50 g/1.75 oz egg white
50 g/1.75 oz butter
50 g/1.75 oz flour
50 g/1.75 oz sugar
20 g/0.66 oz chopped lavender
stencil of triangle, 15 cm x 6 cm/6 in x 2.33 in

Pascal Jalhaij

'New dishes come to me every day.'

Restaurant Vermeer

Prins Hendrikkade 59-72

1012 AD Amsterdam

T 020 55 64 885

F 020 55 64 858

vermeer@nh-hotels.nl

www.restaurantvermeer.nl

Pascal Jalhaij: 'I started working here as chef three years ago. That first year we lost our only Michelin star; but in the two years after that, we earned two back.

'Vermeer has always had an excellent kitchen. Now I've lent that a certain contemporary swing. The real creating actually happens between the furnace, meaning the stove, and the *passe*. I design the dish on the plate. And I always do that in a way that no one would ever consider mashing it all together with a fork. Even though the flavour's the thing, I still consider it important to keep people fascinated with the dish itself, and so I pay a great deal of attention to the visual aspects.

'I often go to the visual arts for inspiration: Picasso, Dali. That's also the way I worked on the recipes for this book. A black-and-white chequered tile floor from Johannes Vermeer found its way to the plate in the form of a "Beef marrow and brioche chessboard". A still life containing a book gave me the idea for a "Mille-feuille of thinly sliced apple".

New dishes come to me every day. When I arrive in the kitchen in the morning, the cooks can tell from the way my hair looks whether I've had a restless night. When I can't sleep, it means I've written down a lot of ideas. I ask my staff to try out certain things for me. They reserve an hour for that every day. Everyone has to be finished by six o'clock: then I assemble all the different elements, and from that we make a dish together. We taste it, and make sure

Pascal Jalhaij

the wine stewards are there so they can start thinking about a suitable wine right away. If it's good, we go on to perfect it. I keep track of the best ideas, and they're added to menu, which we refresh four times a year. In addition to our daily work, our kitchen also has that dynamic element of new dishes all the time.

'Of course a big kitchen requires a certain amount of discipline. But I don't act like a tyrant. If you do that, the discipline is not self-generated. I try to command discipline through my own creativity, and make sure that everyone has their own responsibilities. I'm very keen on having people think along with me. Every day there are nine young people in the kitchen, backed up by even younger work-students and apprentices. I expect four days of complete dedication from my people. That's leaves them one day to sleep in, and two days for a bit of social life.'

Grilled duck liver on brandied apricots

with a veil of cream

Gerard Ter Borch II (1617-1681), **Girl in peasant costume** *(c. 1650).*

The woman depicted in this painting is probably the painter's half-sister, Gesina Ter Borgh, also an artist. She is dressed in a peasant costume, and her hairstyle complete with red ribbon was typical for an unmarried peasant woman. The paper she is holding in her hand is probably the text of a play or poem. The unspoilt country life of shepherds and farmers was extolled and idealized in seventeenth-century cultural circles. The elite also built pleasure gardens and summer homes in the Het Gooi region, on the Vecht River and around the Lake of Haarlem. But the country life led at these summer residences was hardly comparable to the drudgery of actual rural life.

Duck liver and goose liver were already enjoyed by the ancient Romans. Pliny the Elder (23/24-79 AD) wrote about this subject in one of the 37 books of Naturalis historia, where he mentions the controversy about who came up first with the idea of eating goose liver. Pliny couldn't make up his mind: it was either the consul Scipio Metellus or M. Sestius, 'by his birth a gentleman of Rome'. One of the two was: 'the first inventor of this great good and singular commodity to mankind'.

ingredients for 4 servings

4 slices duck liver, about 100 g/3.5 oz each
160 g/5.66 oz white bread, diced small
50 g/1.75 oz butter
50 g/1.75 oz sugar
1.5 dl/5 fl oz unsweetened cream, whipped stiff

Combine the diced bread with the butter and sugar. Place the mixture into 4 round moulds with a diameter of 6 cm/2.33 in and bake in the oven for 6 minutes at 180°C/356°F.

Grill the slices of duck liver evenly on both sides. Then roast them briefly in the oven at 180°C/356°F. Season the duck liver with white pepper and sea salt.

Just before serving, place the duck liver on the baked bread mixture and top the liver with a generous tablespoon of whipped cream.

Beef marrow and brioche chessboard

with cold oxtail bouillon and verbena

Johannes Vermeer (1632-1675), **The love letter** *(1667-1669).*

A woman holding a cittern (a string instrument with a pear-shaped body, related to the lute) in her hands receives a letter from the maid. She is a well-to-do woman, judging by her clothes and the interior of the room. The marble-tiled floor, which we know so well from these intimate scenes of Vermeer and other Delft painters such as Pieter de Hooch, served as an inspiration for Restaurant Vermeer's starter. One might assume that any self-respecting seventeenth-century home would have had such a floor, but the opposite was true: research conducted by C.W. Fock has revealed that floors with marble tiles laid in geometric patterns were a rarity in those days. Only very occasionally could such a hall or vestibule be found, because preference was generally given to the cosier (and warmer!) wooden floor.

ingredients for 4 servings

for the brioche

20 thin slices of brioche, 2 cm x 2 cm/0.75 in x 0.75 in

for the marrow

16 thin slices of beef marrow, rinsed, 2 cm x 2 cm/ 0.75 in x 0.75 in

fine sea salt

freshly ground white pepper

zest of 1 lemon

for the bouillon

1 kg/2 lb 3.33 oz ox tails, sawed into small pieces

1 kg/2 lb 3.33 oz beef, cut into small cubes

1 kg/2 lb 3.33 oz beef bones, sawed into small pieces

120 g/4.25 oz carrots

120 g/4.25 oz celery stalks

100 g/3.5 oz onions

800 g/1 lb 12 oz shallots

120 g/4.25 oz leek

100 g/3.5 oz tomato paste

>>

In the Dutch Golden Age, it was customary to use beef marrow for a tart by combining it, for example, with powdered sugar, cinnamon, ginger, diced veal and raisins. Or the marrow was melted and sautéed, and then sugar, egg yolks and crushed almonds were added. After that, it was encased in a dough crust and baked.

The bouillon Preheat the oven to 200°C/392°F. Place the ox tails, cubed beef and beef bones in the oven until they become dark brown in colour. Sauté carrots, celery, onion, shallots and leek in a large frying pan and add the tomato paste. Deglace with red wine and let it condense to a syrupy consistency. Now add the browned bones and fill the pan with water to cover. Bring to the boil and skim the foam off the surface with a skimmer. Add the parsley stems, coriander seeds, bay leaves, sea salt and white pepper corns and let the bouillon simmer for about 3 hours on a low fire. Remove the pan from the heat and let the bouillon rest for half an hour to extract the gelatine from the bones. Strain the bouillon carefully through a cloth. Reduce this clear bouillon on a low fire until you have obtained the taste desired (be sure the bouillon is very concentrated, since it loses a lot of its taste when served cold). Place the bouillon in the fridge and keep ice-cold.

The marrow Bring a generous amount of water to the boil, add the sliced marrow and cook for 1 minute. Rinse immediately with cold water. Cook the sliced marrow once again for 1 minute in plenty of water, and rinse again immediately with cold water. Season the marrow slices with fine sea salt, freshly ground white pepper and lemon zest.

3.5 dl/12.33 fl oz red wine
parsley stems
crushed coriander seeds
bay leaves
coarse sea salt
white pepper corns
verbena

The brioche Toast the brioche in the oven or toaster.

The presentation Arrange a chessboard on a large plate, alternately composed of 3 x 3 slices of marrow and toasted brioches. Fill a piping bag with a very fine nozzle (3 mm/0.125 in) with the jellied (stiffened) bouillon and squirt a circle 12 cm/4.75 in in diameter on the plate. Garnish the jellied bouillon edge with verbena.

Mille-feuille of thinly sliced apple

with marinated mackerel and a yoghurt-red beet vinaigrette

ingredients for 4 servings

for the mille-feuille

16 sheets puff pastry, 8 cm x 14 cm (3.125 in x 5.5 in)

4 Granny Smith apples

for the vinaigrette

500 g/1 lb 1.5 oz yoghurt

2 tbsp roasted hazelnut oil

0.5 dl/1.75 fl oz champagne vinegar

4 dl/14 fl oz red beet juice, reduced to a syrup consistency

for the mackerel

4 mackerel fillets about 60 g/ 2 oz each

olive oil

5 dl/17.5 fl oz white wine

30 g/1 oz finely sliced young carrots

60 g/2 oz thinly sliced shallots

1 sprig thyme

>>

The hard, green Granny Smith apple was named after Maria Ann Smith (1799-1870). She was given the nickname 'Granny' because of the loving care she had given as a midwife to newborn babies and mothers in her neighbourhood. Granny Smith was an Englishwoman who in 1838 moved to Australia with her husband and children as colonists. In Eastwood, she grew all sorts of fruit in their backyard. Not far from a brook that ran through their property, she noticed a variety of a wild French apple growing there spontaneously. In 1868, Granny let her neighbours sample the apples. They were so enthusiastic about these tasty apples that they started to cultivate them as well. It still took until 1890 for the apple to gain nationwide fame. Five years later, the Granny Smith apple was exported for the first time. Today, it is one of the world's best-selling apples.

The mackerel Bring the white wine to the boil and add the thinly sliced carrots, shallots, thyme, bay leaves, parsley and crushed pepper corns and let it all steep like tea for 45 minutes. Brush the mackerel fillets with olive oil and pour the hot marinade over them. Simmer gently at about 75°C/167°F. Leave the mackerel to cool in the liquid.

The mille-feuille Preheat the oven to 180°C/356°F. Bake the pastry for 20 minutes until it puffs up (bulges). Peel and core the apples and cut them into very thin slices.

Jan Lievens (1607-1674), **Vanitas still life** *(1628-1630).*

The books in this still life inspired Restaurant Vermeer to create a puff pastry recipe. Puff pastry is an invention of Claude Gellée (c. 1600 - 1682), better known as the French seventeenth-century painter Claude Lorrain. A magnificent landscape drawing by this artist can be seen at the Rijksmuseum in Amsterdam. Lorrain knew early on that he wanted to become a painter, but to earn money he started to work for a confectioner at the age of twelve. Legend has it that a few years later he decided to bake some special bread for his sick father. He folded butter into a sheet of dough, which he repeatedly folded and flattened. In the oven, the dough developed into an airy pastry consisting of countless layers. Instead of receiving gratitude, Lorrain was dismissed. But his invention lives on, just like his art.

The vinaigrette Use a hand blender or mixer to combine the yoghurt, hazelnut oil and champagne vinegar into a smooth dressing.

The presentation Build up the dish as follows: place a sheet of baked puff pastry in the centre of a large plate, cover with the thinly sliced apples, pat the marinated mackerel dry and arrange on top. Place another sheet of puff pastry on top, and cover again with apple and mackerel. Repeat once more and finish with a sheet of puff pastry. Before serving, surround the mille-feuille with the yoghurt vinaigrette, 'marbling' it with the reduced red beet sauce.

4 bay leaves

4 sprigs parsley

crushed pepper corns

salt

Boudin blanc of chicken

with Oosterschelde lobster and a spinach sauce

Johannes Vermeer (1632-1675), **The kitchen maid** *(known also as* **The milk maid** *(c. 1658).*

Myriad ideas exist about the painting's meaning (moderation, worldly love, faith), but little about what the woman is doing. She is pouring milk from an earthenware jug into a bowl. There is bread on the table. Perhaps the woman is preparing some bread mush, a dish consisting of milk and bread, which was not only eaten for breakfast, but often also for supper with the warm meal. For people who were poorly off, this type of food usually constituted the most important source of nutrition.

ingredients for 4 servings

for the chicken

100 g/3.5 oz chicken

50 g/1.75 oz pork fat

1 dl/3.5 fl oz milk

1 slice white bread

10 g/0.33 oz **pain de mie** (inner crumbs) of brioche

1 shallot, chopped

5 g/1 tsp salt

3 dl/10.5 fl oz whipping cream

1 egg

2 g/0.5 tsp potato starch

200 g/7 oz Oosterschelde lobster tail, cleaned and cooked

white pepper

salt

1 clove garlic, crushed

>>

Boudin noir is originally black pudding, but in this recipe Restaurant Vermeer makes a white pudding, inspired by the white skin of Vermeer's milk maid. An eighteenth-century cookbook provides a recipe for 'White pudding, how you should make it'. This recipe used 'the meat of two large, fat capons' or 'three hens'. This boudin blanc or white pudding could also be fried.

The chicken Mix the chicken, pork fat, milk, white bread, *pain de mie*, shallot, salt, egg and potato starch in the food processor until it becomes a smooth, homogenous mass. Finally, add the cream. To prevent curdling, cook at moderate heat. Season the mixture with white pepper, sea salt and crushed garlic. Rub the mixture through a sieve and add the lobster. Using a piping bag, squirt out long rolls about 2 cm/0.75 in in diameter. Cut the rolls into pieces 7 cm/2.75 in in length and wrap up in heatproof plastic foil. Cook these 'sausages' for 20 minutes in hot water (but don't let them boil) and remove the plastic wrap. Now fry the white pudding in fresh butter until golden brown all round and serve in the sauce.

The sauce Bring the white wine, fish stock, garlic and shallot to the boil and reduce to half its volume. Stirring constantly, add the cold, diced butter. Add the spinach to the sauce and purée with a hand blender. Strain the sauce through a fine-meshed sieve and whip up with the hand blender until foamy.

for the sauce

1 dl/3.5 fl oz white wine

1 dl/3.5 fl oz fish stock

0.5 clove garlic

1 finely chopped shallot

50 g/1.75 oz raw spinach, washed

50 g/1.75 oz cold butter, diced

ER. wat bu-ten maat be-staat, int on-maats
qaat ver-ghaat.

Mousse of caramelized walnuts

with roasted hazelnuts and macadamia nuts

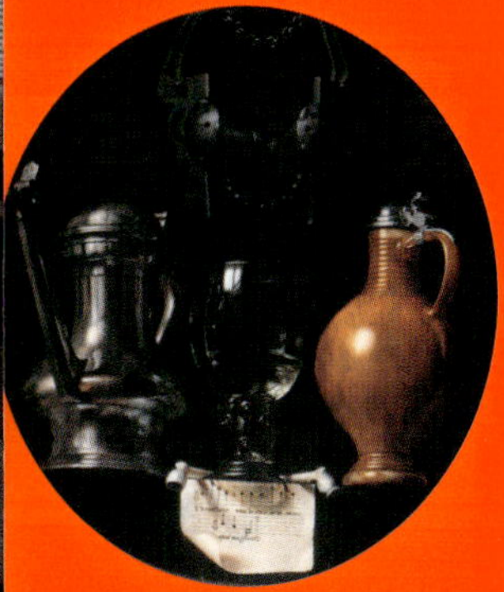

Torrentius (pseudonym of Johannes Simonsz. van der Beeck) (1589-1644), **Emblematic still life with flagon, glass, jug and bridle** *(1614).*

Water was rarely drunk in the seventeenth century. It is nevertheless assumed that what we see depicted in the painting is a wine flagon to the left and a water jug to the right. The water was used to dilute the wine to obtain the desired taste. However, in those days the drinking water in the Dutch cities was usually too polluted for consumption. Or too salty, because in 1540 the Amsterdam canals (which were directly connected to the Zuyder Zee via the IJ) were already so brackish that brewers could no longer use the water to brew their beer. The strangest plans were devised to supply the city with fresh water. For example, the painter and architect Jan de Bray (c. 1627 - 1697) developed a blueprint for a basin about 200 m x 200 m/218 yds x 218 yds with walls 7 m/ 23 ft high, which he planned to fill with water brought in by ships. This huge reservoir was supposed to have been built on the Amstel, in the vicinity of today's Weesperplein.

The Nutcracker Suite inspired Restaurant Vermeer to create this nut dessert. Nut trees — contrary to other edible plants — are ancient. That's why they can be found in the New as well as the Old World. Macadamias were initially native only to Australia. Although it was suspected that Aboriginals did eat the nuts, their edible properties (and tastiness) were only discovered in the late nineteenth century. Hawaii is the world's largest producer of macadamia nuts today.

ingredients for 4 servings

150 g/5.33 oz walnuts
50 g/1.75 oz roasted hazelnuts
50 g/1.75 oz roasted macadamia nuts
50 g/1.75 oz granulated sugar
2 tbsp lime juice
2 sheets gelatine
2 dl/7 fl oz whipping cream
2 tbsp brown rum

Place the granulated sugar in a small saucepan and melt on low heat until it becomes a golden brown caramel. Add the walnuts. Caramelize them briefly and pour the mixture onto greaseproof paper to cool. When the sugar has become crisp, use a knife to cut the caramel into small, uniform pieces. Dissolve the soaked gelatine in 0.75 dl/2.5 fl oz of the cream and add the nut mixture as well as the brown rum. Whisk the rest of the cream to the consistency of yoghurt and gently fold it into the mixture. Leave it to cool thoroughly and serve the mousse in a coupe glass topped with roasted hazelnuts and macadamia nuts.

Raw mackerel tartar

with a mint and red pepper dressing and crisply fried smelt

Master of the Amsterdam Bodegone, ***Kitchen piece (Bodegone)*** *(1610-1625).*

'Bodegone' is the Spanish name for kitchen piece, but the original meaning of 'bodegón' was inn. Impressed by the kitchen pieces of Aertsen and Beuckelaer, Velazquez (1599 - 1660) also painted various inn scenes and kitchen pieces. Evidently, Holland's warning finger has been incorporated in this painting: the cook is surrounded by the most delectable foods (including two smoked mackerel) as well as playing cards and money, but he presents us only with a humble soup...

ingredients for 4 servings

for the tartar

200 g/7 oz mackerel fillet, skinned and boned

3 sprigs broad-leaved parsley, finely chopped

1 spring onion, finely chopped

1 shallot, chopped

freshly ground pepper and salt

for the dressing

10 mint leaves, finely chopped

1 mild chilli pepper, seeded, thinly sliced

1 dl/3.5 fl oz farmer's yoghurt

juice of 0.5 lemon

0.25 dl/1 scant fl oz ginger syrup

1 dl/3.5 fl oz olive oil

freshly ground sea salt

for the smelt

arachide oil (peanut oil) for deep frying

50 g/1.75 oz smelt

100 g/3.5 oz flour

freshly ground pepper and salt

Only day-fresh fish should be used for raw preparation. Fresh fish does not smell like fish but like the sea and can be recognized by the fish's crystal-clear eyes and bright red gills. If mackerel is not in season (winter), you can take red bream (dorade) or sea bass. Be particularly careful with mackerel, because it's a fish that spoils rather quickly. That was the reason why in seventeenth-century England, mackerel was one of the few foodstuffs merchants were allowed to sell on Sundays.

The tartar Cut the mackerel fillet into small cubes. Add the finely chopped broad-leaved parsley, spring onion and chopped shallot. Season with pepper and salt.

The dressing Use your food processor or hand blender to blend the finely chopped mint, chilli pepper, yoghurt, ginger syrup and lemon juice to a smooth consistency. Then slowly add the olive oil and season the mixture with freshly ground sea salt.

The smelt Dry the smelt with kitchen paper and season with pepper and salt.

Mix the smelt with the flour. Shake off the excess flour, for example in a sieve, and deep fry the smelt in the arachide oil for about 2 minutes at 180°C/350°F until crisp. Drain the smelt on kitchen paper.

The presentation Place a ring with a diameter of 6 cm/2.33 in on a plate. Press one quarter of the tartar firmly into the ring. Remove the ring and dribble the dressing decoratively round the tartar. Surround the mackerel tartar with the crisply fried smelt. Chop the mint leaves very finely. Sprinkle a few slivers of mint and freshly ground pepper over the tartar and the starter is ready to be served. Repeat this process for the other three portions.

Marseillaise

Mediterranean fish soup

ingredients for 4 servings

for the fish stock (hearty bouillon)

0.5 dl/1.75 fl oz olive oil

1 kg/generous 2 lb fish bones without heads (lean types of fish such as turbot, sole, halibut and brill)

0.5 leek

0.5 onion

0.5 fennel

0.5 celery stalk

bunch of parsley

3 cloves

8 crushed pepper corns

2 bay leaves

1.5 litres /scant 2.5 pt water

2 dl/7 fl oz Noilly Prat (dry Vermouth)

for the rouille (a type of garlic sauce)

1 egg yolk

10 g/scant 0.5 oz bread crumbs

0.5 chilli pepper, seeded, finely sliced >>

A somewhat simpler fish soup used to be eaten frequently during religious fasts. In 1522, the philosopher Erasmus campaigned against the complex fasting regime that established what should — and especially what should not — be eaten on certain days. For a great part of the year it was forbidden to eat meat, so people ate fish. Erasmus disliked the system because the poor could not afford to buy fish, whereas the rich over-indulged. Erasmus quoted (with approval) the words of Jesus: 'That what goes into the mouth defiles not the man.'

The fish stock Finely chop the leek, onion, fennel, celery stalk and parsley. Rinse the fish bones well with cold water and dry them with kitchen paper. Heat the oil in a large, tall pan. Sauté the finely chopped vegetables and herbs in the oil until soft but not coloured. Add the fish bones and deglace the pan with Noilly Prat. Add the water and bring to the boil. Skim the foam off the liquid as it develops. Let the fish stock simmer for 20 minutes without boiling. Strain the fish stock through a fine-meshed sieve.

The rouille Blend egg yolk, bread crumbs, chilli pepper, lemon juice, saffron, mustard and garlic in the food processor until you get a thick, smooth paste. Add the olive oil, a drop at a time, and season the rouille with freshly ground salt.

The croûtons Prepare the croûtons by thinly slicing the French bread. Rub the bread with garlic, sprinkle with olive oil and bake in the oven until crisp.

Gabriël Metsu (1629-1667), **Woman having a meal,** *known* **as The cat's breakfast** *(1660-1667).*

A woman in a simple indoor setting, breakfasting on bread and herring. She gives the bone to the cat. The simplicity of the woman and the interior contrasts sharply with the vase of carnations and tulips, which in those days were a precious — if temporary — possession. Having fish for breakfast was not uncommon in the seventeenth century. People ate salt herring or fried fish. In the sixteenth century, smelt was even called 'breakfast fish'

- juice of 0.5 lemon
- 4 saffron threads
- 2 tsp mustard
- 4 cloves garlic
- 2.5 dl/8.75 fl oz olive oil

for the croûtons

- a few pieces of French bread
- olive oil
- garlic

for the fish soup

- 0.5 dl/1.75 fl oz olive oil
- 2 cloves garlic, minced
- 30 g/1 oz leek, finely sliced
- 30 g/1 oz shallot, finely chopped
- 50 g/1.75 oz fennel, finely chopped
- 20 g/0.66 oz celeriac, finely chopped
- 6 ripe, peeled tomatoes, cut into pieces
- 1 tsp thyme or rosemary, chopped
- 1 tsp grated orange zest
- 4 saffron threads
- 150 g/5.33 oz fish fillets (gurnard, cod, hake, whiting, red mullet or dab; select seasonal fish that are not too expensive)
- freshly ground pepper and salt
- a few drops Pernod (a Marseille aperitif with the taste of anise)
- 12 clams (washed and pried open with a knife); instead of clams, use other shellfish, such as mussels or cockles
- Gruyère

The soup Cut the fish fillets into finger-size pieces. Half of the fish will be used for the garnish on the plate (use the most attractive pieces of fish for this purpose), and the other half will be used to thicken the soup. Heat the olive oil in a large, tall pan. Add the garlic, sliced leek, chopped shallot, fennel, celeriac, thyme, rosemary and saffron, and sweat them gently until lightly coloured. Add the fish fillets and tomatoes and braise until the vegetables are done. Add the fish stock and bring everything to the boil. Leave it on a low heat for about 10 minutes. Purée the soup in the food processor or with a hand blender. Season the soup with freshly ground pepper and salt and a few drops of Pernod.

The presentation Take deep soup plates and rub them with a few drops of olive oil. Place the reserved pieces of fish fillet and the clams on the plates and put them in a 100°C/212°F preheated oven for 3 minutes until the fish is almost done. Ladle the hot soup onto the fish and sprinkle with fine spring onion rings.

Serve with rouille, croûtons and gruyère to make the dish complete.

Grey shrimp croquettes

and a cream sauce with mustard and green herbs

*Aert van der Neer (1603/4-1677), **River view by moonlight** (c. 1650).*

Fishing was an extremely important source of income in the seventeenth century. Around 1650, nearly half a million people in Holland worked in fishing, whereas today the number has declined to less than 20,000. They fished the North Sea, the Wadden Sea and the Zuyder Sea, where they caught eel, anchovies and herring. Herring was the most important catch and called the 'Great Fishery'. But people also fished in rivers, as can be seen on the atmospheric painting by Aert van der Neer. Even though this fisherman is working with nets, in those days most freshwater fish were caught on the line and therefore rather expensive.

ingredients for 4 servings

for the cream sauce

- 10 g/0.33 oz tarragon, finely chopped
- 10 g/0.33 oz broad-leaved parsley, finely chopped
- 10 g/0.33 oz chervil, finely chopped
- grated zest of 0.5 lemon
- 2 tbsp coarse mustard
- 2 tbsp crème fraîche
- 2 tbsp ginger syrup
- freshly ground pepper and salt

for the croquettes

- 30 g/1 oz butter
- 30 g/1 oz flour
- 30 g/1 oz shallot, chopped
- 1.5 dl/5 fl oz fish stock (see Starter)
- 1.5 dl/5 fl oz whipping cream
- 2 eggs, beaten
- 150 g/5.33 oz grey shrimp
- 1 sprig tarragon

>>

The French have an expression for conceited people: 'se croire le premier moutardier du pape' ('he thinks himself the pope's head mustard-maker'). This expression has its origin in the fourteenth century when Pope John XXII hired his nephew to fill this important post. It is not clear whether the pope created this sinecure to give his rather useless nephew something to do, or whether the pope was a mustard enthusiast. In those days, the pope's seat was in Avignon. Even though mustard was already known in ancient China and Egypt, France is nevertheless the mustard country par excellence. Thanks to the mustard from Dijon, such as Grey Poupon, a brand founded in 1777.

The cream sauce Mix the tarragon, chervil, lemon zest, mustard, crème fraîche and ginger syrup and season with salt and pepper.

The croquettes Melt the butter, add the flour and stir until it becomes a smooth paste (roux). Cook the roux for 2 minutes, stirring constantly, without letting it take on colour. Continue stirring, while adding the cold fish stock and the cream until, the sauce is thickened. Add the lemon zest, the finely chopped parsley and tarragon. Let the mixture cool for 10 minutes. Add the shrimp last (otherwise they become tough), season with salt and pepper, and let the mixture cool in the fridge for 4 hours. Take the mixture from the fridge and, using your hands, form into croquettes. Roll the croquettes through flour, dip into the egg mixture and then roll

them through the coarse breadcrumbs. To keep them from falling apart during frying, dip them again in the egg mixture and roll them once more in the breadcrumbs. Deep fry the croquettes in hot oil at a temperature of 180°C/350°F.

Deep fried tarragon and parsley can be used as a garnish. Be careful when frying herbs because the high moisture content can cause the oil to sputter. Keep at a safe distance. Drain the herbs on kitchen paper and season with salt.

5 sprigs parsley

grated zest of 0.5 lemon

freshly ground pepper and salt

coarse breadcrumbs

Baked flat Zeeland oysters

served on goose liver risotto

ingredients for 4 servings

for the risotto

30 g/1 oz butter

30 g/1 oz shallot, finely chopped

150 g/5.33 oz risotto rice

3 dl/10.5 fl oz poultry bouillon

2 tbsp Madeira wine

50 g/1.75 oz cold, cubed goose liver

freshly ground salt and pepper

for the oysters

12 flat Zeeland oysters

100 g/3.5 oz flour

30 g/1 oz butter

Zeeland oysters are a local variety. Oysters have been cultivated in Zeeland only since the end of the nineteenth century; before that time, 'wild' oysters were eaten. Even though seventeenth-century paintings always show raw oysters, they were also served baked, just as in this VisaandeSchelde recipe. They can also be found on a menu prepared in the Middle Ages for banquets attended by earls and noblemen. It happened to be a day of fasting, therefore no meat was put on the table. The baked oysters constituted part of the first course and were accompanied by dishes such as wine soup, pea soup with pickerel liver, all sorts of egg dishes (including boiled eggs baked into an apple cake), cooked salmon, pike, sturgeon and carp, pickerel sausages, baked bream and lobster pasty.

The risotto Melt the butter in a tall frying pan or fireproof casserole. Add the finely chopped shallots and sauté until soft without colouring. Add the risotto rice and stir until the grains turn glassy. Add the bouillon and Madeira and bring to the boil, stirring constantly. Place the lid on the pan, turn down the heat to low and let the rice simmer gently for about 20 minutes. Remove the lid from the pan and carefully blend in the cold, cubed goose liver. Season with freshly ground pepper and salt.

Abraham Mignon (1640-1679), **Still life with oysters and fruit** *(c. 1660-1679).*

Provided they have been kept chilled on ice, oysters stay alive on land for two weeks, and therefore fresh. Already in the Middle Ages, oysters were eaten only in months containing an 'R'. In Dyet's Dry Dinner *(1599) the British writer William Butler wrote: 'It is unseasonable and unwholesome in all months that have not an R in their name to eat an oyster.' And much later the song writer Stoddard King (1889 - 1933) rhymed in* The Man Who Dared:

'Let's sing a song of glory to
Themistocles O'Shea,
Who ate a dozen oysters on
the second day of May.'

The oysters Place an oyster on a folded tea towel, hold it firmly in one hand, and carefully pry the oyster open with a special oyster knife. Repeat until you have opened all the oysters. Dry the oysters on kitchen paper and then roll them in flour. Melt the butter until foamy and fry the oysters on both sides until golden brown and crisp.

The presentation Rinse 12 beautiful oyster shells until thoroughly clean and place them in an oven preheated to 100°C/212°F for 5 minutes. Cover the plates with coarse sea salt or the seaweed provided with the oysters. Divide the warm oyster shells over the plates. Spoon some creamy goose liver risotto into the shells and top with golden, crisply fried oysters. Serve with a lemon wedge.

Buttermilk mousse

with quince compote and spiced gingerbread strips

Martinus Nellius (worked 1673-1706), **Still life with pears, medlar and glass** *(c. 1674-1706).*

King Francis I of France (1494-1547) was so fond of cotignac, biscuits made of baked quince puree, that he sometimes ate them with tears of joy in his eyes. The French culinary historian Maguelonne Toussaint-Samat relates how 'François' paid an unannounced visit to his mistress, Mme. d'Étampes. He brought along cotignac to enjoy together with her. When he entered the room, he realized immediately that another lover was hiding in it. He left the room, but not without first sliding the delicacy under the bed with the words: 'Here you are, Brissac, everyone has to live.'

The quince compote that VisaandeSchelde prepares here is an age-old recipe. Quince has been used for centuries for making jelly, compote, jam and marmalade. The word marmalade is derived from the Portuguese 'marmelo' meaning quince. Marmalade was therefore originally quince jam.

ingredients for 4 servings

for the mousse

- 2 dl/7 fl oz buttermilk
- 2 dl/7 fl oz semi-stiff whipped cream
- 40 g/1.5 oz powdered sugar
- 3 sheets gelatine
- juice of 1 lemon

for the compote

- 3 quinces
- 50 g/1.75 oz sugar
- 1 dl/3.5 fl oz water
- zest of 0.5 lemon
- juice of 0.5 lemon

The mousse Soak the sheets of gelatine in cold water until soft. Remove and squeeze out any excess water. Heat the lemon juice, add the softened gelatine and stir until the gelatine is dissolved. Mix the buttermilk with the powdered sugar, and gently fold the dissolved gelatine and the semi-whipped cream into the mixture. Divide the mousse over four large wine glasses, and let it stiffen in the fridge for at least 1 hour.

The compote Peel the quinces, cut off the flesh along the core and cut into small pieces. Put the flesh in a saucepan and add the water, sugar, lemon zest and juice of 0.5 a lemon. Cook over low temperature for 15 minutes until soft. Cool the compote in the fridge. Spoon the quince compote over the mousse and serve.

The spiced gingerbread Cut the spiced gingerbread into long, wafer-thin strips. Place the strips on baking paper and dry them for 1 hour in an oven preheated to 75°C/167°F. Cool them and stick a few strips into the mousse immediately before serving, otherwise they become tough.

Deep fried gambas in beer batter

Adriaen van Ostade (1610-1685), **Dancing couple** *(c. 1625-1640).*

The man to the right drinks his beer from a so-called 'pasglas' (pass glass). The Rijksmuseum has a rare specimen of a pass glass in its collection. Although these glasses are very special now, in the sixteenth and seventeenth centuries they were quite common. Beer was drunk from these glasses by people of all walks of life. The glass filament that winds around the outside of the glass and divides it into more or less equal parts, gives the glass its name: because in the Middle Ages the Dutch word 'pas' meant measure. Engraved on a pass glass exhibited in Vienna, Austria, are the rhymed rules of a game which can be summed up as follows: players took turns trying to drink exactly from one stripe to the next. If they failed, they had to continue drinking to the following stripe.

Beer was the most important beverage for the crew of a VOC (Dutch United East India Company) ship. We can deduce from the handbook Nieuwe Hollandsche Scheeps-Bouw *(New Dutch Shipbuilding), dating from that period, what sort of provisions were taken on board a ship with a crew of a hundred men who were away for a year: 2,000 litres Spanish wine, 600 litres French wine, 900 litres brandy, 12,000 litres 'thin' beer, 600 litres 'good' beer, 22,500 litres water (1.14 litres = 1 quart). Additionally, every man was allowed to take along a cask of brandy at own cost. The longer the journey, the worse the water got. Since the crew ate a lot of salted foods, they suffered considerable thirst aboard the ships. When adding up all the beverages, the result is hardly more than a generous litre of liquid per man per day.*

ingredients for 4 servings

for the gambas

8 shelled gambas (large shrimp) with tail

for the salad

lettuce

dressing

for the batter

3 dl/10.5 fl oz beer (1 bottle)

2 eggs

pinch of salt

pinch of curry powder

275 g/9.75 oz flour

Heat the deep-fry pan to 180°C/356°F. Combine the beer, eggs, salt and curry powder in a bowl. Add the flour by sieving it into the bowl and whisk everything together until it becomes a smooth batter. Don't whisk too long or the dough will get tough. Dip the gambas in the batter up to the tail, and then fry them in the deep-fry pan for 4 to 5 minutes. Dress the salad, arrange on the plates and top with 2 gambas per person.

Potato soup with truffles

Jan Havicksz. Steen (1626-1679), **The parrot cage** *(1660-1670).*

A little boy is feeding a cat with a spoon from an earthenware jar; most likely, porridge or 'sop'. It would be tempting to assume that the Dutch word 'sop' means soup, but this would be incorrect. It referred to a kind of mush or gruel cooked in a kettle, hence the name 'kettle meal': the broth in which the meat had been cooked above the fire was thickened with bread. Potato soup was not eaten at all in the seventeenth century. Even though potatoes, which were a novelty from the New World, threatened to become trendy in the sixteenth century, it took until the nineteenth century for them to appear on the tables of both the masses and the elite.

The truffle is surrounded by myth. For centuries, people believed that the truffle was 'born' during thunderstorms, when lightning struck the ground. Actually, truffles are mushrooms that grow underground on the roots of trees, particularly oaks. Because space is limited round the roots, the taste of these stinkhorns (the family they belong to) is highly concentrated. The darkest, nearly black variety, grows mainly in France; white truffles are primarily found in Italy. Together with Spain, these two countries are the most important suppliers of truffles. Each of the two countries furnishes some 50 tons (112,000 lb) of truffles a year. For comparison's sake: more than 1,500 tons (3,360,000 lb) of gold are extracted every year. That's why one kilogram of truffles can cost thousands of euros.

ingredients for 4 servings

250 g/8.75 oz peeled potatoes

5 cloves garlic (peeled)

1 litre/35.25 fl oz whipping cream

salt

fresh truffles

Cook the potatoes with the garlic and salt until tender. Drain well. Mash the potatoes with a potato masher. Add the cream and bring the mixture to the boil. As soon as it starts to boil, use the hand blender briefly to give the soup a more airy texture.

Grate fresh truffles over the soup and serve immediately.

Côte de boeuf with a sauce of roast garlic

Paulus Potter (1625-1654), **Four cows in a meadow** (1651).

In his short life, Paulus Potter immortalized Dutch cattle in all its glory. Hardly any of these numerous magnificent breeds still exist. If you happen to see grazing cows in the Netherlands today, they usually are Holstein cows, a type of species bred in America and Canada in the nineteenth century, and originally descendants of the Frisian dairy cow, an eighteenth-century breed that is as rare today as the seventeenth-century Groningen Whiteheaded (Blaarkop) or Dutch Belted (Lakenvelder) Cattle.

ingredients for 4 servings

côte de boeuf (prime rib, sirloin of beef), about 800 g/1 lb 12 oz

salt and pepper

1 bulb garlic

2 dl/7 fl oz red wine

2 dl/7 fl oz veal stock (from a jar)

oil

clarified butter

Côte de boeuf is a sirloin of beef. One of the most persistent misconceptions circulating about beef steak is that the meat first needs to get a solid crust to ensure that the juices do not escape. In his book Meteorologica, *the philosopher and scientist Aristotle wrote more than three centuries before Christ: 'When the pores contract, the moisture contained in the object can no longer escape, but is locked into the closed pores.' In the nineteenth century, the German chemist Von Liebig provided 'scientific' proof of this theory, and even the great chef Escoffier thought that by searing the meat, its taste would be better preserved. But in reality, searing actually adds taste to the meat thanks to a browning process!*

The garlic Place the garlic on an ovenproof plate, sprinkle with a few drops of oil and put it in the oven preheated to 200°C/392°F. Leave the garlic bulb in the oven until tender. Then squeeze the cloves out of the bulb into a saucepan. Place the pan on the burner and deglace immediately with red wine. Reduce the wine to one third, then add the veal stock. Reduce until it has the thickness of a sauce.

The côte de boeuf Preheat the oven to 250°C/482°F. Season the côte de boeuf with salt and pepper. Sear the meat in (clarified) butter, then place it in the preheated oven for about 20 minutes. Remove the meat from the oven and let it rest for 20 minutes.

After the meat has rested, cut it into neat slices and return it to

the oven for 1 minute prior to serving.

Delicious with mashed potatoes and stir-fried vegetables with a touch of crushed garlic.

M.D.H

Sautéed goose liver with raspberry sauce

Melchior d'Hondecoeter (1636-1695), **The philosophizing magpie** *(1660-1695).*

This is one of the many hunting scenes that were hanging in what is today known as 'Soestdijk Palace' until the end of the eighteenth century. Soestdijk was originally a country estate built for the Amsterdam mayor Cornelis de Graeff around 1650. It was acquired by Stadholder William III in 1674 as a hunting seat. After William married Mary Stuart and was crowned king of England in 1688, he had more stately accommodations built in the Veluwe, namely Het Loo Palace. In those days, the Veluwe, now a national park, was still 'wild and desolate'. An Englishman described it in those days as follows: 'one of the best hunting Countries in ye World but good for Little else'. The type of hunt William preferred to organize was a large-scale par-force hunt, with horsemen pursuing large game. William III died in 1702 after a fall from his horse, which had stepped into a molehill.

Foie gras (fat liver) is mainly known as a starter. Often it is accompanied by a sweet wine. This is a custom that might have its origins in the fact that goose liver used to be served as a dessert or before the dessert. In the seventeenth century, desserts were extremely diverse: from cheese with bread, cake or tart, to fruit and confit of herbs. But dishes we might consider rather strange as dessert fare today were then also consumed to conclude a meal: braised vegetables and white bread stew.

ingredients for 4 servings

- 125 g/4.5 oz raspberries
- 3 tbsp honey
- 2 dl/7 fl oz veal stock (from a jar)
- glass of port
- 320 g/11.33 oz goose liver for sautéing, about 80 g/2.75 oz per person
- salt and pepper

The sauce Heat the honey in a saucepan until hot, then add the raspberries (reserve 8 to 10 berries for finishing the sauce) and deglace the mixture with a glass of port. Add the veal stock and cook the sauce for about 2 minutes. Strain the sauce. Just before serving, add the reserved raspberries to the sauce so they remain nice and whole.

The goose liver Special goose liver intended for sautéing is best purchased from the finer restaurants in your area. Other goose liver tends to become deflated because a lot of fat melts off during cooking and hardly anything is left over. Sauté the livers in a hot frying pan and season with salt and pepper. The liver is done when you are able to insert a fork into it with virtually no resistance. Serve the goose livers on a plate, surrounded with the sauce.

Asparagus mousse with confit of asparagus

Gerard van Honthorst (1590-1656), ***The merry fiddler*** *(1623).*

The glass this cheerful musician is holding in his hand — in a work by Utrecht painter Gerard van Honthorst — is called a 'berkenmeier'. With its cylindrical foot and knob-like ornaments (knops), and the funnel-shaped goblet, it might have been the precursor of the rummer, a glass very similar in appearance but with a bucket bowl. The knops first had the shape of thorns and later of blackberries. Initially, the purpose of these knops was to ensure that the glass did not easily slip out of a person's greasy fingers.

Riesling is both the name of a grape and a specific wine made from these grapes. The origin of Riesling, the king of grapes, can be traced back to the mid-fifteenth century. A lot of Rhine wine is made from the Riesling grape, and in the seventeenth century a great deal of Rhine wine was consumed in the Netherlands. This Rhine wine was more acidic than the French wines. The Dutch word 'rins' (sour) is derived from: 'Rhijnse wijn' (Rhine wine) and changed in the course of time into 'rinse wijn' (sour wine).

ingredients for 4 servings

10 stalks white asparagus

5 dl/17.5 fl oz Riesling wine

5 dl/17.5 fl oz whipping cream

200 g/7 oz sugar

14 g/0.5 oz gelatine

fresh nutmeg

Take note that this dessert has to stiffen in the fridge for 4 to 5 hours. Peel the asparagus, and cook 8 stalks in a generous amount of water, together with 100 g/3.5 oz of sugar. When the asparagus stalks are tender, strain and purée them. Stir in the gelatine that was soaked in cold water and leave the mixture to cool. Meanwhile, whip the cream with 50 g/1.75 oz of sugar until it reaches the thickness of yoghurt. Pour the mousse into moulds and place them in the fridge for 4 to 5 hours.

Before serving, thinly slice the remaining two asparagus and put them in a dry, hot frying pan. Add 50 g/1.75 oz sugar, keep moving the pan around until the sugar has dissolved and caramelized. Scoop the asparagus pieces from the pan; be careful, they are very hot.

Unmould the mousse onto the plates and divide the asparagus pieces around the mousse. Grate a little nutmeg over the top and serve.

Joost de Bruijn & Michiel van der Eerde

'We try to offer something for every taste.'

Restaurant Supperclub

Jonge Roelensteeg 21

1012 PL Amsterdam

T 020 344 64 00

F 020 344 64 05

info@supperclub.nl

www.supperclub.nl

Joost de Bruijn: 'Michiel and I both began here in 2000. I started in the restaurant business when I was just a kid, and I've had jobs everywhere, including as assistant chef in restaurants with Michelin stars. I had just decided to leave Holland for a trip around the world, to write a book about fusion cooking, when they asked me to come here as chef.

'Our menu has a lot of variety, and we try to offer something for every taste. We serve a maximum of 160 meals in an evening. From the dining room, the guests can see us dressing the plates. The combinations are unique, but not too complex. Not dozens of flavours on a plate. We have a global kitchen: we really cook everything, from all over the world. We use forgotten Dutch vegetables like parsnip, but we also bring in our pak-choi cabbage from far away. We can adapt our menu every day to what our suppliers offer.

'We do crazy things. For example, we've served ashtrays filled with creme brulée and chocolate cigarettes. We like to put our guests on the wrong track, but we do that with respect; what they find in that ashtray has to be perfect and delicious.'

Michiel van der Eerde: 'Even when I was quite young, I knew I wanted to work in the kitchen. So, when I was about sixteen, I applied at a restaurant in Maarsen that had a Michelin star. Almost before I knew it, cooking was all I could think about. After that I worked at a few famous places. But at a certain point I discovered that I didn't want to spend sixteen hours a day hovering

Michiel van der Eerde and Joost de Bruijn

over plates just to earn a Michelin star. When Joost asked me to come and work here, I agreed right away.

'We cook one daily menu, with special exceptions for vegetarians and people with an allergy. The plates almost always come back to the kitchen completely empty. That makes you feel good. Joost and I work one day a week together, and we switch off for the rest of the week. Together we come up with what we're going to make.

'The guests here lie on beds and watch performances while a DJ plays music. That concept also defines our role. We'll serve salmon tartare and toast with latex gloves. After ten minutes, everyone's eating with gloves on. People get involved, and they remember us.'

Langoustine carpaccio

with a salad of white asparagus and fresh herbs, served with a vanilla-grapefruit vinaigrette

ingredients for 4 servings

for the carpaccio

12 fresh langoustines

for the salad

8 white asparagus

2 sprigs tarragon

2 sprigs dill

2 sprigs chervil

100 g/3.5 oz purslane

for the vinaigrette

2 grapefruit

1 vanilla pod

0.5 dl/1.75 fl oz ginger syrup

1.5 dl/5 fl oz crustacean stock

2 dl/7 fl oz corn oil

freshly ground pepper and salt

Langoustine carpaccio. The name carpaccio is associated with the painter Vittore Carpaccio (1457 - 1526). However, the dish itself is not nearly as old. The story goes that in 1950 the chef of Harry's Bar in Venice served a dieting customer very thinly sliced, raw beef fillet which he called 'Carpaccio', because when the diner inquired about the name of the creation, the chef looked outside where he saw an eye-catching poster announcing an exhibition of the painter's work.

The langoustines Clean the langoustines, remove the head and break the shell off the tail. Don't forget to remove the black vein. Place 3 langoustine tails per person between plastic wrap or grease-proof paper. Flatten them with a cleaver to obtain nice, round-shaped carpaccio.

The vinaigrette Mix the juice of 1 grapefruit, the crustacean stock, ginger syrup, seeds of the vanilla pod, salt and pepper and slowly add the corn oil. Whisk constantly until the vinaigrette is creamy and smooth.

The salad Peel the asparagus and cut them into thin strips using a vegetable peeler. Combine the asparagus strips with the washed purslane and the herbs. Mix with 0.5 of the vinaigrette.

Adriaen Coorte (c. 1683- after 1707), **Still life with asparagus** *(1697).*

Why did Adriaen Coorte paint this bunch of asparagus? Some see the phallic shape of the vegetable as a sexual innuendo, and indeed, for centuries asparagus has been a symbol of male sexuality. On the other hand, it has also been a cherished vegetable because its white colour defies the darkness of winter. The English historian Simon Schama contends that Coorte wanted to demonstrate the simplicity of this vegetable, since asparagus was looked upon as food for the poor in the seventeenth century. Hans Faverey (1933-1990) wrote the following verse about the work of Coorte, who also painted several outstanding fruit still lifes:

'Not a breath of wind,
the absence of something:
beating steadily

in gooseberry, raspberry,
the creamiest of asparagus.'

The presentation Brush 4 plates with the remaining vinaigrette. Arrange a few herbs decoratively on the plate. Next, transfer the carpaccio in one brisk movement onto the plate; the herbs are now visible through the translucent carpaccio, creating an attractive contrast. Sprinkle the carpaccio with salt and pepper, and arrange the salad in the centre. Finally, section the grapefruit by cutting along the skin of the fruit with a sharp knife, removing all the membranes. Garnish the salad decoratively with the grapefruit sections.

Salad of crisply fried duck leg confit

with maize vinaigrette and popcorn

Melchior d'Hondecoeter (1636-1695), **A pelican and other birds near a pool***, known as* **The floating feather** *(c. 1680).*

No matter how exotic the ducks to the right of the pelican may look, most of them are still regular visitors to the Netherlands today, for example, the small teal on the left, the red-breasted goose in the centre and the shelduck (second on the right). Melchior d'Hondecoeter painted the birds from live models found in the menageries of country estates, or in his own hennery. The exotic birds were not only for show (and splendour), but they were also consumed. This canvas was painted for William III's hunting seat, today known as Soestdijk Palace.

ingredients for 4 servings

for the duck legs

2 duck legs, 300 g/10.5 oz each

8 dl/28 fl oz goose fat

1 sprig rosemary

1 sprig thyme

0.5 bulb garlic

zest of 1 orange

salt and pepper

2 sprigs broad-leaved parsley, chopped

1 clove garlic

40 g/1.5 oz butter

for the salad

100 g/3.5 oz raw duck liver

200 g/7 oz mixed salad leaves (radicchio rosso, frisée, oak leaf and lamb's lettuce)

1 corncob

for the vinaigrette

2 shallots, finely chopped

20 g/0.66 oz Savora mustard (sweet)

10 g/0.33 oz honey

1.5 dl/5 fl oz corn oil >>

Confiting is an age-old technique aimed at preserving products for a long period of time. From a seventeenth-century manuscript containing more than seventy recipes for confit of fruit, herbs and flowers, it can be concluded that in those days these sugared foods were frequently used for medicinal purposes. It is also possible to confit food in fat, as is the case with this Supperclub duck recipe, which is a modern version of the classic confit de canard.

The duck legs Confit the duck legs - together with the rosemary, thyme, 0.5 bulb of garlic, the orange zest, salt and pepper — in a pan with goose fat at a slow 80°C/176°F. After about 1.5 hours, the duck is cooked to the bone. Take the duck from the fat and remove the skin. Debone the duck, taking care that the pieces are equal in size and not too small. Fry the duck pieces in a non-stick pan until crisp. Then add the butter, chopped shallot, crushed garlic, chopped parsley, some pepper and salt.

The salad and the vinaigrette Tear the lettuce into bite-sized pieces and wash thoroughly. Cook the corncob al dente, and then sauté it in a non-stick pan until golden brown. Let it cool, then cut the corn off the cob. Cut the duck liver into small cubes. Stir the chopped shallot, apple, mustard, honey, vinegar and apple juice with the corn oil until smooth. Add the chopped chives and corn and season with pepper and salt.

The popcorn Fry the dried corn in a deep pan containing hot oil, add pepper and salt, and heat until it pops. Remove the popcorn immediately from the pan and drain on kitchen paper.

The presentation Mix the lettuce with the cubed duck liver and half of the vinaigrette. Arrange on the plates. Top the salad with the fried duck. Finish off with the remaining vinaigrette, the popcorn and some chervil.

0.5 Elstar apple, peeled and cored
0.5 dl/1.75 fl oz apple cider vinegar
0.5 dl/1.75 fl oz apple juice
salt
freshly ground black pepper
10 g/0.33 oz chopped chives

for the popcorn

30 g/1 oz dried corn
oil
pepper
salt
some chervil

Tabbouleh with Dutch shrimp, mint, tomatoes, coriander and parsley

served with an oyster shooter

Clara Peeters (1589-after 1657), **Still life with fish, oysters and shrimp** *(1607-1650).*

The Antwerp painter Clara Peeters can be considered one of the first artists to paint fish still lifes. Here we see an eel, a perch, several shells, oysters and shrimp, among others. In the seventeenth century, one of the methods of catching shrimp was by means of nets that were dragged through the sea by horses. People also sailed along the coast in hookers, dragging a fine-meshed net — a so-called trawl — along the seabed.

Tabbouleh is a couscous dish from the Middle East and North Africa. Couscous is a grain product. The type of flour used depends on the geographical location. The couscous sold in the Netherlands is usually semolina (wheat). The name is derived from the Berber word 'seksou'. In some local African languages the name couscous means 'food'. Just as in some European countries the word 'bread' is synonymous with 'eating'.

ingredients for 4 servings

for the tabbouleh

- 90 g/3 oz couscous
- 160 g/5.5 oz small Dutch shrimp
- 2 pomodori tomatoes
- 20 mint leaves
- 6 sprigs broad-leaved parsley
- 2 spring onions
- juice of 1 lime
- 0.5 dl/1.75 fl oz almond oil
- 15 g/0.5 oz sumac (an herb made of the sour berries of the velvet sumac)

for the shooter

- 4 creuse oysters
- 1.2 dl/4.5 fl oz lime vodka
- Tabasco

- 12 leaves of washed Little Gem (also called lactuca, a soft type of lettuce)

The tabbouleh Soak the couscous in 1 dl/3.5 fl oz of water until the water is absorbed. Skin the tomatoes and quarter them lengthwise. Remove the seeds and cut them into cubes.

Finely chop the parsley and mint, and slice the spring onions into thin rings. Mix the couscous with the tomatoes, chopped herbs, spring onions, lime juice, the sumac and the almond oil.

The shooter Carefully remove the oysters from the shells and make sure there is no shell grit attached to the oysters. Place an oyster into each of the 4 shot glasses and cover it with lime vodka. Finish off with a touch of Tabasco.

The presentation Place the Little Gem leaves on a beautiful large platter and spoon the couscous on top of the lettuce. Garnish it with the Dutch shrimp and place the shot glasses on the platter.

Roast fillet of lamb's neck

with sea lavender, broad beans and peas, accompanied by baked Opperdoes potatoes and basil-laced lamb sauce

Paulus Potter (1625-1654), **Shepherds and their herd** (1651).

Mutton and lamb constituted an important component of the Spanish hotchpotch. This dish, although considered typically Dutch by many, has its origin in Spain. When the city of Leiden was liberated on 3 October 1574, which ended the siege by the Spaniards, a pot of hotchpotch was supposedly found in the deserted enemy camp. Actually, the hotchpotch did not resemble today's version in any way, because it contained neither carrots nor potatoes. Most likely it was spicy meat with onions, and parsnips. Whatever the story: all of Leiden still eats hotchpotch on 3 October to commemorate the event. And also herring and white bread, because that was the food the liberated people of Leiden finally got to eat again.

ingredients for 4 servings

for the lamb's neck

4 lamb's neck fillets, 180 g/6 oz each
100 g/3.5 oz butter

for the vegetables

100 g/3.5 oz sea lavender
120 g/4.5 oz shelled peas
120 g/4.5 oz shelled broad beans
2 sprigs summer savoury
freshly ground salt and pepper

for the sauce

2 lamb shanks
0.5 winter carrot
1 leek
150 g/5.33 oz celeriac
2 shallots
1 bulb garlic
2 sprigs thyme

>>

Lamb shanks come from the lowest part of the leg and are frequently used to make soup or a hearty bouillon. Rosemary is an herb often used in the preparation of lamb. In the seventeenth century, rosemary was an herb symbolizing eternity. Joost van den Vondel described in a moving poem how a girlfriend of his deceased little daughter Sara 'braided a wreath of rosemary out of love for her best mate'.

The sauce Cook the lamb shanks until golden brown. Cut the carrot, leek, shallots, celeriac and garlic into 1.5 cm/0.6 in cubes. Wash the vegetables and add to the lamb shanks. Then add 2 litres/70.5 fl oz of water and bring to the boil. Skim off the foam as the water starts to boil, and reduce the liquid until half of it has evaporated. Add the red wine, thyme, rosemary, bay leaves, crushed pepper corns and 4 sprigs of basil and continue reducing until 2 dl/7 fl oz are left. Strain through a sieve and add 100 g/3.5 oz of butter. Season with salt and pepper.

The potatoes Wash and dry the potatoes. Sprinkle them with salt and wrap them in aluminium foil. Bake the potatoes in the oven for about 20 minutes.

The lamb's neck Sauté the lamb neck fillets in butter until they are nice and rosé inside: about 3 minutes on each side. Remove them from the pan and let them rest.

The vegetables Blanch the peas and broad beans for 2 minutes and continue to cook them in a pan with butter. Add the summer savoury and the sea lavender and season with salt and pepper.

The presentation Remove the foil from the potatoes and divide them over the plates. Place the cooked vegetables in the centre and top with the sliced lamb fillets. As a finishing touch, add the sauce and finely sliced basil leaves.

2 sprigs rosemary

4 bay leaves

10 crushed pepper corns

5 sprigs basil

0.5 litre/17.5 fl oz red wine

200 g/7 oz butter

for the potatoes

12 small Opperdoes potatoes

salt

Pineapple granité

with tempura-fried bananas and mango sushi

ingredients for 4 servings

for the granité

150 g/5.33 oz sugar

1.5 dl/5 fl oz white wine

1 pineapple

1 star anise

1 clove

for the bananas

4 peeled apple bananas; save the peels

100 g/3.5 oz tempura flour

Chinese spice mix (cloves, star anise, pepper, fennel seed and cinnamon)

for the sushi

100 g/3.5 oz Japanese sushi rice

40 g/1.5 oz powdered sugar

1 dl/3.5 fl oz milk

1 dl/3.5 fl oz water

seeds of 1 vanilla pod

1 ripe mango

1 sushi mat (a bamboo place-mat; fat-free paper is an alternative)

In this recipe, the Supperclub mixes rice with powdered sugar, an ingredient already known in the seventeenth century. The cane sugar derived from the colonies was refined in a Dutch 'Suyckerbackerij' (a sugar-baker's shop or sugar refinery): enterprises that are considered to have been one of the first forms of industry. During the refining process, products such as powdered sugar, white sugar and syrup were produced through evaporation with the help of lime, clay, eggs and ox-blood.

The gratiné Peel and core the pineapple. In a food processor or blender, purée the pineapple into a pulp and strain. Bring white wine, sugar, star anise and a clove to the boil. Let it simmer for 10 minutes and strain through a sieve. Now blend with 2 parts of pineapple juice and 1 part of sugar wine. Pour the mixture into a container and put it in the freezer.

The rice Bring the rice with the milk, water and vanilla seeds to the boil. The rice is done when the liquid has evaporated. Then blend the sugar into the rice. Peel and thinly slice the mango. Take a sushi mat and cover it with some plastic wrap; this prevents sticking. Spread the rice evenly over the plastic wrap (about 1 cm/0.4 in thick), then cover with the thinly sliced mango. Roll up and cut the roll into 8 slices.

Albert Eckhout (c. 1610–c. 1666), **East-Indian market stand** *(1640–1666).*

This market stand displays a variety of local fruits: rambutan, mangostan, copra, mango, grapefruit, pineapple and bananas. The red fruits in the centre are durians from Malaysia. The latter have an extremely hard shell with razor-sharp prickles. The fruit weighs about 2 kg/4.5 lb and grows on trees that can become 30 m/100 ft tall. According to the culinary historian Alan Davidson, 'death by durian' is not an uncommon occurrence. Davidson claims that the fruit is equally loved and hated. This can be attributed to, among other things, the penetrant odour released by the durian, and its equally heavenly flavour. Enjoy your meal!

The bananas Mix the flour with water until you have a smooth paste: it shoul d be about the consistency ofyoghurt. The batter has to be used immediatel y, so it can't be prepared in advance. Peel the bananas and dip them first into the Chinese spice mix, and then into the tempura batter. Fry them at 170°C/338°F until they are nice and crisp. Drain on kitchen paper.

The presentation Put the bananas decorativel y back into the peel s and pl ace them on the pl ates, al ong with 2 pieces ofsushi. Take the granité fom the feezer and scoop out attractive curl s with a spoon. Serve the gratiné shavings in a shot gl ass with the dessert.

Sources consulted

Given the nature of this book, I decided against listing — book by book — the library of titles that proved helpful to me. The list below provides the most important sources and might serve as a guide for people wishing to read more about certain subjects. I limited myself to the books available in English-language editions. For a more complete bibliography, please refer to the Dutch edition of this book.

If you are interested in preparing an authentic festive meal as served during the Dutch Golden Age, immerse yourself in *De verstandige kock* dating from 1667. This cookbook, popular at the time, was translated into English by Peter Rose as *The Sensible Cook* and is available via his site www.peterrose.com, among others. English translations of several of these recipes can be found on Marleen Willebrands' site www.kookhistorie.com. This site also contains English information about recipes from the first printed Dutch cookbook *Een notabel boecxken van cokeryen*, as well as Carol Battus' *Eenen seer schoonen ende excellenten Cocboeck* from 1593. Another site concentrating on the history of Dutch cuisine is www.coquinaria.nl.

Furthermore, I used the Folio Society's edition *Dumas on Food* (a selection from Alexandre Dumas' posthumously published *Le Grand Dictionaire de Cuisine* from 1873, translated by Alan and Jane Davidson) and *The Curiosities of Food* (1859) by Peter Lund Simmonds, in Alan Davidson's edition from 2001.

M.F.K. Fisher translated *Physiologie du Goût* (1825) by Jean-Anthelme Brillat-Savarin as *The Physiology of Taste* — a book still able to tantalize our taste buds two centuries on.

An interesting and entertaining historic text about (the catching of) fish is *The Compleat Angler* by Izaak Walton from 1653, which is still available today.

Gerard Dou (1613-1675) painted himself with an open book around 1650.

The culinary reference work I used most frequently when writing this book was *The Penguin Companion to Food* (2002, originally published in 1999 as *The Oxford Companion to Food*) by Alan Davidson. In more than a thousand pages, he covers the history of everything edible, all arranged into readable, informative and often humorous entries listed in alphabetical order. A must-have for anyone interested in culinary history. Alan Davidson had considered writing the preface to *The Rijksmuseum Cookbook*, but sadly he passed away in December 2003.

Less complete and practical than Davidson's encyclopaedia, but equally humorous, is the anecdotic *Histoire naturelle et morale de la nourriture* by Maguelonne Toussaint-Samat, which was published in English as *History of Food*.

Also worthwhile reading are *All Manners of Food* by Stephen Mennell, about the different French and English gastronomic cultures since the Middle Ages, and *Savoring the Past* by Barbara Ketcham Wheaton about the history of French cuisine.

And if the above books leave you with a taste for more, you can always turn to *The Cambridge World History of Food* by Kenneth F. Kipple and Kriemhild Coneè Ornelas, a wealth of information presented from a scientific point of view, which is most likely to stifle just about any cook's desire to become creative in the kitchen. The two boxed volumes are so thick they can easily serve as a kitchen stepstool.

The prophetess Anna reading a book. *Some believe that she is the mother of the man who made this painting in 1631, Rembrandt Harmensz. van Rijn.*

In his worthwhile standard work *On Food and Cooking*, Harold McGee has written about the technical and physical backgrounds of food and cooking processes. If you start leafing through *Larousse Gastronomique*, you feel an immediate urge to head for the kitchen.

For people who simply want to know everything, and for those who are curious to find out what an aduki tree looks like, *The Visual Food Encyclopedia* by François Fortin is an indispensable source of information. A clear and richly illustrated encyclopaedia that presents not only all sorts of facts about more than a thousand foodstuffs from all over the world, but also offers basic recipes.

Johan Huizinga is considered the greatest historian the Netherlands has ever brought forth. His concise *Dutch Civilisation in the Seventeenth Century* is still the best introduction to that era,
but unfortunately it can only be found in antiquarian bookshops.

The Dutch Republic by Jonathan Israel is a good book for anyone interested in delving deeply into the seventeenth century. *Dutch Primacy in the World Trade*, by the same author, deals with Holland as a trading nation.

Unrivalled is *The Embarrassment of Riches* by Simon Schama, a study of the Dutch mentality in the seventeenth century.

The Netherlands, as seen through the eyes of foreigners, is the subject of *Touring the Low Countries*, in which Kees van Strien collected myriad travel accounts from British people who had visited the Netherlands in the period between 1660 and 1720. The book also includes excellent records.

The Tulip by Anne Pavord contains a well-documented chapter on the Dutch tulipomania.

Anyone wishing to gain insight into life on a Dutch East India Company (VOC) ship should read *Batavia's Graveyard* by Mike Dash, a book in documentary form but nonetheless highly suspenseful. It also provides information about the mysterious painter Torrentius.

Everything about prices and the value of paintings can be found in *Art at Auction in 17th Century Amsterdam* by the economist John Michael Montias, who also wrote Johannes Vermeer's biography. Together with John Loughman, John Michael Montias also co-authored a book about the interior of seventeenth-century houses (and particularly about the place of paintings within that setting): *Public and Private Spaces*.

Art & Home is a magnificently illustrated book by Mariët Westermann, that bears the self-explanatory subtitle *Dutch Interiors in the Age of Rembrandt*.

A great deal of information about life in the upper classes can be found in *Picturing Men and Women in the Dutch Golden Age* by Klaske Muizelaar and Derek Philips.

The 17th-Century Doll's Houses of the Rijksmuseum by Jet Pijzel-Dommisse supplies extensive information about these great museum attractions.

The website http://emblems.let.uu.nl/emblems/html/index.html of the Emblem Project Utrecht provides a number of emblem books in facsimile and their English translations, along with comprehensive explanations and sources.

In *Still Life with a Bridle*, the Polish writer Zbigniew Herbert gives his interpretation of the work by the mysterious painter Torrentius and his vision of the Dutch Golden Age (with a chapter on the tulip craze).

In describing the paintings, I primarily relied on the unrivalled website of the Rijksmuseum: www.rijksmuseum.nl. Naturally, paintings should ideally be seen in real life, but sitting behind the computer in the comfort of one's home looking at all the paintings containing oysters is also very satisfying indeed.

The standard work par excellence about seventeenth-century Dutch painting is *The Golden Age* by B. Haak.

A standard work about still lifes, already half a century old, is *Dutch Still-Life Painting* by Ingvar Bergström. *Still Lifes: Techniques and Style* (edited by Arie Wallert) delves more deeply into technical aspects as well as scientific research into still lifes.

Sam Segal wrote a book that treats all sorts of aspects of seventeenth-century still lifes: *A Prosperous Past*.

Jan Havicksz. Steen (1626-1679),
The feast of St. Nicholas
(1665-1668)

The large loaf of gingerbread in the basket was called a 'hylickmaker'. 'Hylick' means marriage. A man usually presented such a cake to a woman when he proposed to her. If she ate a piece of the cake, it meant she accepted his proposal. The cake is also related to St. Nicholas. According to legend, he helped to save three unmarried sisters from prostitution by offering them a dowry, which enabled them to get married. The saint was often depicted with three gold coins that make reference to this anecdote. Even the name 'good merry man' could be a corruption of 'good marriage man'.

Index of recipes

intermediate course I

main course

intermediate course II

dessert

pies

colophon

publisher Thomas Rap, Amsterdam

illustration editors Bert Natter and Jan Martin Wilschut

lay-out Valérie Starink van der Ooyen / Amsterdam Hotsprings

typesetting Paul van Kuik / Amsterdam Hotsprings

fonts Dolly (Underware) and DIN

lithography Litho Spirit, Amsterdam

printing Hooiberg, Epe

translation Sam Garrett (essay and interviews) and Dagmar Speer (recipes)

cover illustration Floris Claesz. van Dijck (ca. 1575-1651), *Still life with cheeses* (1615). Rijksmuseum Amsterdam. Portrait author: Nienke Katgerman

with thanks to Ronald de Leeuw, Jolien Schuerveld, Paulien Retèl, Paulien Kintz, Maud Soethout, Carina Greven, Madeleine ter Kuile, Henk van Os, Diederik van Vleuten, Karin Evers, Jan van der Bijl, Mara Grimm, Jan Borst, Toon Verhoeven (Antiquariaat Bavink), Wilma Schuhmacher and Max Schuhmacher (Antiquariaat Schuhmacher), Jan van Schooten, Geurt Naber and Paul Brandt.

www.therijksmuseumcookbook.com

ISBN 90 6005 486 5
NUR 440